THE
NATURAL HISTORY
MUSEUM

. . . .

Nature's Treasurehouse

JOHN THACKRAY
AND BOB PRESS

PUBLISHED BY
THE NATURAL HISTORY MUSEUM, LONDON

First published by The Natural History Museum,
Cromwell Road, London SW7 5BD
www.nhm.ac.uk/publishing
© The Natural History Museum, London, 2001
ISBN 0 565 09164 6

Edited by Karin Fancett
Designed by David Mackintosh
Reproduction and printing by Craft Print, Singapore

Distribution:
Australia and New Zealand
CSIRO Publishing, PO Box 1139
Collingwood, Victoria 3066, Australia

UK and rest of the world
Plymbridge Distributors Ltd.
Plymbridge House, Estover Road
Plymouth, Devon PL6 7PY, UK

foreword 6

preface 8

acknowlegements 9

1. ORIGINS OF THE MUSEUM: ... 11
Sir Hans Sloane and his collection

2. THE MUSEUM ESTABLISHED: ... 23
Montagu House

3. A NEW BUILDING: ... 37
The Bloomsbury development

4. TO SOUTH KENSINGTON: ... 55
The great divide

5. THE COLLECTIONS: ... 69
Building the treasurehouse

6. EXHIBITIONS AND EDUCATION: ... 93
Reaching the audience

7. RESEARCH: ... 109
Unravelling mysteries

8. THE DIGITAL AGE: ... 127
Into the future

bibliography 140

index 142

FOREWORD

Few out of the millions of people who visit The Natural
History Museum in South Kensington each year realize that the
exhibitions and galleries around them are only a fraction of what
the Museum has to offer. The Museum's imposing cathedral-like
architecture and its famous displays – whether of dinosaurs,
of the blue whale and its relatives, of gems or of human biology –
are but the front door to an extraordinarily important scientific
research institution. Behind the scenes lies one of the world's
finest collections of natural objects – some 70 million animals,
plants, minerals, rocks and fossils drawn from virtually every
country on earth. These collections are the focus of vital research
for the Museum's world-renowned team of scientists and for
thousands of scientific visitors who work with them each year.

Since its origins as a founding part of the British Museum,
The Natural History Museum has always had a very important
double role: it carries out both scientific research, and it communi-
cates the results of that research through its exhibitions. This book
charts the history of both of these activities clearly and concisely
from the origin of the Museum in 1753 through to the present day.
Now is a particularly important time in the Museum's history
for such a book to appear. The Museum is on the threshold of a
very significant change, as a result of which the two sides of its
activities will be brought together. Through the building of the
new Darwin Centre at the Museum, the vast collections and the
work of the scientists will be there for all to see – our science will
be accessible to all.

This splendid short history of the Museum was the idea and
creation of John Thackray, formerly the Museum's Archivist.
Sadly he did not live to see its completion, but it serves as a fitting
testament to his great knowledge and love of The Natural History
Museum, and of its rich history. I hope it will give much pleasure
and enlightenment.

Sir Neil Chalmers
Director, 2001

PREFACE

As befits one of 'nature's treasure houses', The Natural History Museum has featured in a variety of previous books, including at least one full history. This short history is intended to fulfil a very different purpose.

The idea for a small volume giving a readily accessible account was John Thackray's. He envisaged a work which chronicled the more important milestones in the development of the Museum, but which also brought to life the times in which they occurred, and the excitement and sometimes controversy which surrounded many of these events. For contrary to common prejudice, Museums can be exciting places, especially those like The Natural History Museum, which are at the pinnacle of their particular areas of expertise.

As first a geologist, and later the Archivist at the Museum, John was ideally placed to translate his idea into reality. His deep interest in and knowledge of the history of the Museum and natural history as a whole enabled him to select appropriate episodes, while his keen appreciation of the circumstances and personalities involved with particular events, and an eye for the more whimsical aspects of Museum life, enabled John to tell the story in his own distinctive style.

The manuscript was well under way when, sadly, John died. My role has been to take up the threads and complete the remaining chapters. Discrepancies in style are the product of this mid-stream change of authors. Any enjoyment derived from reading this book is to John's credit; any mistakes are mine.

John's intention was to portray the Museum warts and all. A place frequented by the great, the good, the average and the odd; where plans have been inspired and sometimes distinctly flawed; but whose heart – if an institution can have such an organ – is in the right place and whose efforts over the years have proved worthwhile.

Bob Press
2001

ACKNOWLEDGEMENTS

Numerous individuals have contributed to this book but several
are deserving of special mention. They include: Susan Snell and
Vicky West for much help with archival work; Drs Bob Bloomfield,
Chris Jones, Angela Milner and Tony Shelley for information
on their research specialities; Prof. Chris Humphries and Dr David
Williams for sharing their knowledge and interest in Museum
history. Also John Thackray's many friends and colleagues at
the Museum who gave advice, excavated data and checked facts
at my request. Finally John himself, whose idea this was and
whose efforts played the greatest part in bringing the project to
completion.

CHAPTER 1

ORIGINS OF THE MUSEUM:
SIR HANS SLOANE AND HIS COLLECTION

Hans Sloane was one of the great men of early 18th-century London. He was wealthy, he was popular, he lived in a large house in Bloomsbury, and was doctor to much of high society. Sloane was also well known in the international world of science. He was in touch with naturalists and philosophers all over the world, people who would report their discoveries to him and send him their books, and treat him with deference and respect.

Sir Hans Sloane, shown at the age of 76. This copy of a portrait by Stephen Slaughter hangs in the Board Room of The Natural History Museum.

Things had not always been like this, for Sloane was a man of humble origins. He was born at Killyleagh, Co. Down, Ireland, on 16th April 1660, and attended the village school. He became interested in natural history as a boy, recording later in life that he had from his youth "been very much pleas'd with the study of plants and other parts of Nature". He moved to London to study medicine when he was nineteen, and after four years went abroad to complete his studies. He and two friends worked in Paris for three months, then he obtained the degree of Doctor of Physic at the University of Orange, where he was greeted "with great applause", and studied at the University of Montpellier. When Sloane returned to London in 1684 he found time for both botany and the practice of medicine, and became a pupil of Dr Thomas Sydenham, one of London's best known doctors. He was on the first rung of a ladder that was to lead him to the top of his profession.

At about this time Sloane had a great opportunity that he seized with both hands, and which altered the course of his life. He was offered the post of personal physician to Christopher Monk, 2nd Duke of Albemarle, who had just been appointed Governor of Jamaica. He wrote to a number of friends for advice as to whether or not to take the post, and one in particular was persuasive, writing: "Were it not for the danger and hazard of so long a voyage, I could heartily wish such a person as yourself

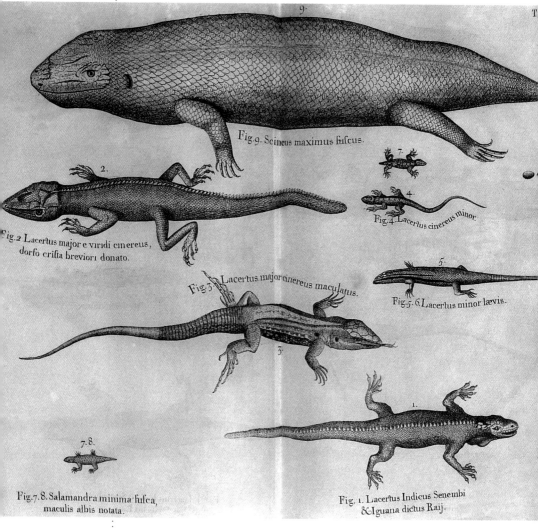

9.

T

Fig.9. Scineus maximus fuscus.

7.

2.

4.

Fig.4. Lacertus cinereus minor.

Fig.2. Lacertus major e viridi cinereus,
dorso crista breviori donato.

5.

Fig.3. Lacertus major cinereus maculatus.

Fig.5. 6. Lacertus minor lævis.

3.

7. 8.

1.

Fig.7. 8. Salamandra minima fusca,
maculis albis notata.

Fig. 1. Lacertus Indicus Senembi
& Iguana dictus Raij.

Illustrations of amphibians, reptiles
and birds from the second volume
of Sloane's work on Jamaica. The
frontispiece described them as being
illustrated for the first time and drawn
"as big as life".

might travel to Jamaica, and search out and examine thoroughly the natural varieties of that island". Sloane spent fifteen months in Jamaica, reporting that "I took what pains I could at leisure-hours from the business of my profession, to search the several places I could think afforded natural productions, and immediately described them in a journal". He returned to England after the sudden death of the Duke, with a rich collection of plants, animals of all sorts, fossils, minerals and earths, and a large quantity of notes and drawings, and found himself famous as a traveller and collector. He married a wealthy widow and set up house in Bloomsbury, where he established his medical practice and started to work over the materials he had brought back with him. Over the years he published papers in the *Philosophical Transactions of the Royal Society,* a catalogue of plants, and eventually the great *A Voyage to the Islands Madera, Barbados, Nieves, S. Christophers and Jamaica ... with the natural history of the ... last of those islands* (2 volumes, 1707 and 1725). Sloane was not a great original scientist – he did not make any fundamental discoveries or develop important theories – but all of these works show his delight in careful description and well-attested fact. He wrote: "The knowledge of natural history, being observations of matters of fact, is more certain than most others, and in my slender opinion, less subjected to mistakes than reasonings, hypotheses and deductions are".

Frontispiece to the first volume of Sir Hans Sloane's account of his voyage to Jamaica and the natural history of the island, published in 1707.

Sloane did not neglect his medical work, and indeed reached the top of his profession with his appointment as Physician in Ordinary to King George II in 1727. He was not a great innovator, basing his diagnoses on careful observation, and avoiding dramatic and drastic remedies. He was unusual in supporting and promoting inoculation, applying it to his own children and to those of the Princess of Wales. He used quinine for the reduction of fever, having bought a large supply of "Peruvian Bark" early in his career, and also promoted the use of milk chocolate "for its lightness on the stomach and its great use in all consumptive cases". His medical and scientific standing, as well as his personal popularity, were recognized by his election as President of the Royal Society in 1727.

SIR HANS SLOANE'S

MILK CHOCOLATE,

PREPARED AFTER THE ORIGINAL RECIPE,

BY CADBURY BROTHERS, LONDON & BIRMINGHAM.

DIRECTIONS:—Put one Ounce of Chocolate (which is two Squares) to a Pint of boiling Milk, or a pint of Milk and Water; add Sugar and Milk as other Chocolate.

. . . .

In England, chocolate was manufactured by a succession of businessmen using Sloane's original recipe. In the 19th century, Cadbury Brothers took over the manufacture.

. . . .

Sloane collected all manner of unusual things, including antiquities, manuscripts and items such as this intricately carved nautilus shell.

However, Sloane the naturalist and Sloane the physician are both eclipsed by Sloane the collector. He had collected and mounted dried plants while a student, and by the time he returned from Jamaica he had accumulated a sizeable museum. In 1691 John Evelyn described Sloane's "universal collection of the natural productions of Jamaica" and mentioned plants, corals, minerals, earth, shells, animals, insects etc. This was the basis on which Sloane built, and for the remaining sixty years of his life he was given, purchased and exchanged individual specimens, collections and whole museums, widening his scope from natural history into antiquities of all sorts, coins and medals, prints and drawings, books and manuscripts, and what we would now class as ethnographic collections. He not only filled his own house with his treasures, but had to buy the one next door as an overflow. His three most important acquisitions were the museum of William Courten (1642–1702) of the Temple, in London; the large botanical collections of Leonard Plukenet (1642–1706); and the huge miscellaneous collection amassed by the apothecary James Petiver (c.1663–1718), which he bought for £4000. This last came to Sloane in a state of disorder, and spurred him on to start to catalogue his own growing museum. He eventually filled twenty-one folio volumes with the details of his natural history collections, mostly in his own handwriting. He recorded the register number, name, locality, provenance and other details of each specimen – an enormous labour for one with so many other calls on his time. These catalogues still make fascinating reading, particularly now that so many of the specimens are lost. The following are some examples from among the natural history collections:

> *253. A piece of the lyons skin that dyed in the Tower in K. James's reign.*
> *141. An ostridges egg from Sir Nicholas Garrards in Essex, smooth. They were eat by the family as other eggs given me by Lady Garrard.*
> *26. A cane made of turned & joined ivory wth ye fig. of a shepherd tempting a naked woman wth an fruit, carved on ye head.*
> *1424. Lapis Tiburonium from Mr Adam from Ireland, a specific for helping women in travail.*

Why did he do it? Sloane expended a large amount of money and an enormous amount of time and effort on his collection. What were his motives? The principal driving force seems to have been a desire to identify and classify the works of nature, and to have examples in his cabinet. He went to great trouble to identify and name his specimens, using the illustrated books in his library, and subjecting his rocks and minerals to both chemical and physical tests. When a new reference book was published he sometimes went back over his specimens to bring their names up to date. Furthering his own profession might be seen as a second motive. Sloane had a strong interest in drugs and remedies of all sorts, and many of his catalogue entries relate to the real or supposed medical powers of the particular object. He was tempted by curiosities and tall tales, but was generally somewhat more critical than many of his contemporaries. In his will Sloane claimed that piety was one of his motives, and suggested that study of his collection would lead to a closer understanding of the wisdom and goodness of God. However, there is little sign that this was important to Sloane as a young or middle-aged man.

. . . .

A Sloane's specimen of Theobroma cacao, *the source of both cocoa and chocolate. His dried plants were mounted in leather-bound volumes.*

As a practising physician, Sloane had a keen professional interest in natural medicinal products and added examples to his collections.

Public museums hardly existed in the 18th century, and so Sloane provided a valuable service in his readiness to welcome visitors. Evelyn's visit in 1691 has already been mentioned, and Sloane's museum was certainly one of the sights of London by 1710, when Zacharias von Uffenbach was received "with vast politeness". Sauveur Morand left a detailed description of a visit to the eleven large rooms comprising Sloane's cabinet in his pair of houses in Bloomsbury Square in 1729. Among the things he noted were "a cupboard where there are 7000 different fruits", and "skins of all sorts of animals". The Swedish botanist Linnaeus came in 1736, but was disappointed to find the renowned collection "in complete disorder", at least in terms of his own system of classification. In 1742, at the age of 82, Sloane retired from medical practice and moved his household and his collections from Bloomsbury to the Manor House in Chelsea, then a village on the western edge of London. His caretaker Edmund Howard provides a hair-raising account of the move, when Sloane's books and "gimcracks" were tossed in at a window of the new house to a man who caught them "as men do bricks". Sloane was visited here by the Prince and Princess of Wales in 1748, after which it was reported: "Their royal highnesses were not wanting in expressing their satisfaction and pleasure at seeing a collection, which surpass'd all the notions or ideas they had formed from even the most favourable accounts of it".

Sir Hans Sloane died at the age of 92, full of years and honour, on 11th January 1753.

Sloane's will was a long and impressive document. First written and signed in October 1739, it had accumulated eight codicils and an unwitnessed note by the time he died. Sloane's aims in writing his will, at least as far as the collection was concerned, were to keep it all together, to ensure that it remained accessible to those who needed and would appreciate it, and to ensure some posthumous fame for himself. To put this into effect he named four executors and some sixty-three trustees, including representatives of his family, noblemen, Members of the House of Commons, Fellows of the Royal Society, bishops, businessmen, antiquaries and naturalists. Their task was to sell the collection intact to the King for the sum of £20,000 if they could, or failing that to offer it successively to the Royal Society, the University of Oxford, the College of Physicians at Edinburgh and various foreign academies. If all else failed then the collection was to be broken up and disposed of piecemeal.

In the end everything went smoothly. The first two meetings of the Trustees were devoted to reading and discussing the will and drawing up a memorial to be presented to the King. This was duly done by the Earl of Macclesfield, who reported to the third meeting on 10th February that the King seemed indifferent, commenting only that he doubted if there was enough money in the Exchequer. The Trustees were undeterred by this set-back, and prepared a petition to Parliament proposing the purchase of the Sloane Collection. The House, being assured that the King was not opposed to the purchase in principle, agreed to debate the matter on Monday 19th March. The three-hour debate convinced the Members that £20,000 was a bargain price for the great collection, and that its annual running cost would be only about £350, and in the end they agreed "that it will be for the honour and advantage of this country to accept of Sir Hans Sloane's legacy". In the course of the debate it was suggested that the Sloane Collection should be united with the Cottonian Library, which had been owned by the nation since 1700, and that the Harleian manuscripts, collected

*Minutes of
the British
Museum General
Meeting 17th
December 1753,
at which the
Trustees allocated
£20,000 of
lottery money to
Sloane's heirs for
his collection.*

17th December 1753   p. 3

Ordered

That the Seal now laid before the Trustees Ingraved with these words, The Trustees of the British Museum, be the Common Seal of this Corporation and continue to be used as Such till another Seal be provided: and that the said Seal be kept in the Custody of the Right Honourable the Lord High Chancellor.

Ordered

That the Sum of £20000. be paid to the Executors of Sir Hans Sloane Bart according to the Act of Parliament of the 26th Year of his Majesty's Reign, in consideration of his Museum or Collection and the Use and Benefit of the Mannor Houses, Gardens and Water at Chelsea mentioned in the said Acts.

Ordered

That the Order upon the Bank for issuing the said Sum of £20000. be in the Form following and that the Common Seal of the Corporation be put to the said Order.

"Pursuant to the Direction of an Act of Parliament
"made in the 26th Year of the Reign of his Present
"Majesty Intitled "An Act for the Purchase of the
"Museum or Collection of Sir Hans Sloane, and of the
"Harleian Collection of Manuscripts and for providing one
"General Repository for the better Reception and more
"Convenient Use of the said Collections, and of the Cottonian
"Library, and of the Additions thereto, We the Trustees of
"the British Museum in a General Meeting Assembled
"Do hereby Authorise and require you, out of the Moneys raised
"by Virtue of the said Acts, and paid into your Hands to
"Issue and pay upon Demand unto the Right Honoble Charles
"Lord Cadogan the Rev: Sloane Elsmere Doctor in Divinity
"William Sloane Esqr and Mr James Empson, being
"the Executors of the said Sir Hans Sloane or unto such
                                                  person

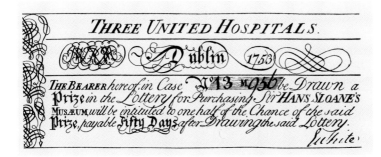

by the 1st and 2nd Earls of Oxford, should be purchased and added. The King was correct in doubting that there was enough money, and it was Speaker Onslow who suggested that the funds to buy and endow the collections and to buy a home for them should be raised by a national lottery.

On Thursday 7th June 1753 King George II attended Parliament to give his assent to the Act that established the Sloane, Cottonian and Harleian collections as the British Museum. The Act established a new Board of Trustees, it laid down that the collection was to be maintained "not only for the inspection and entertainment of the learned and the curious, but for the general use and benefit of the public", and it gave the regulations under which the lottery was to take place. This lottery, which was one of the great scandals of the 18th century, eventually raised just over £95,000 for the British Museum. Of this, £20,000 went to Sloane's heirs, £10,000 to purchase the Harleian manuscripts, £10,000 to buy Montagu House in Bloomsbury, and £30,000 to provide an endowment for maintenance of the British Museum.

Sloane was perhaps not the founder of The Natural History Museum, but his collection and in particular his will was the catalyst that brought the British Museum into being, and thus led directly to the British Museum (Natural History) in 1881 and The Natural History Museum in 1991. His portrait hangs behind the Chairman's seat in the Museum's Board Room, and each of the science departments continues to treasure and make good use of his surviving specimens "for the inspection of the learned and the benefit of the public".

. . . .
Numerous regulations were placed on the lottery but manipulation of ticket sales and other fraud was rife. One of the main culprits was the commissioner appointed by parliament to oversee the scheme.

The Sloane Herbarium

Sir Hans Sloane collected anything and everything of a natural history interest and part of this vast treasury is a remarkable herbarium containing an estimated 120,000 pressed and dried plants. Accompanying this is his collection of "Vegetables and Vegetable Substances", an eclectic assortment of 12,523 seeds, fruits and other items, not all of them of vegetable origin, kept in little boxes. It includes such curios as "A piece of the coffin of Humphry Duke of Glocester" and "A flint found in the middle of an oak at Deptford".

Contemporary drawings accompany some of Sloane's specimens. These often provide clearer details of the actual specimen.

Following the best practice of the day, Sloane kept his herbarium specimens in book-like volumes. The specimens were pasted onto sheets of thick paper that were then stitched and bound together. As many specimens were placed on a page as could be accommodated. There are 338 volumes, ranging in size from quarto to Royal folio, with the largest of them measuring 27 by 18 inches (69 by 46 cm). The preparation of a volume also allowed ample opportunity for confusion, with the initially loose material being mixed up during identification. In 1699 Sloane's contemporary and friend, the botanist John Ray, wrote apologizing for doing just this when naming plants on Sloane's behalf. The specimens were often arranged alphabetically in each volume, which meant long delays while all material for the volume was identified, increasing the chances of disorder. Finally, Sloane's practice of trusting the binder to correctly collate the sheets, with only cursory notes as a guide, seems a somewhat risky course. Any of these factors may have contributed to a number of collections appearing partly in one volume and partly in another.

Sloane himself collected plants in Britain, France and, most notably, Jamaica but these specimens occupy only a few of the 338 volumes. He acquired the remainder of his vast collection by purchase or as gifts, and the people represented include botanists, gardeners, medical officers and ship's surgeons as well as those who, like Sloane, collected the collections of others. The coverage is truly worldwide and many of the collections were among the earliest made from particular regions: Bartram and Catesby from North America, Bulkely from India, Hermann from the Cape, Kaempfer from Japan, and Kamel from the Philippines. Horticultural species from the Duchess of Beaufort's garden at Badminton and medicinal plants from Chelsea Physic Garden also found their way into the herbarium. Such collections are of immense botanical and historical importance.

Sloane was generous in allowing access to his contemporaries, including Carl Linnaeus, who, despite its "complete disorder", proclaimed himself fortunate to have perused the material.

The Sloane Herbarium has been described as being "preserved like an insect in a piece of amber, a wonderful picture of how seventeenth- and early eighteenth-century botanists kept their plants". While this is undoubtedly true, Sloane's herbarium provides far broader and more valuable perspectives than that of long-ago storage methods. The herbarium contains many type specimens, as relevant now as in Sloane's day. It also offers a snapshot of past floras and habitats, and the uses of plants, allowing us to make comparisons with the present and, perhaps, predictions for the future.

. . . .
The "vegetable and vegetable substances" include fruits, seeds, pots of aromatic gums and other items of plant origin. Each numbered box is sealed with beautifully patterned paper.

CHAPTER 2

THE MUSEUM ESTABLISHED:
MONTAGU HOUSE

The Trustees established under the British Museum Act met for the first time in December 1753. Their most pressing job was to find a suitable home for the newly constituted British Museum. After looking at Buckingham House (now Buckingham Palace) and considering putting up a new building in Westminster, the Trustees decided to buy Montagu House in Bloomsbury. This was a spacious and elegant 17th-century mansion, which stood only a short distance from Bloomsbury Square where Sloane had spent most of his life. Even with extensive repairs and alterations, Montagu House was much the cheapest option, and negotiations were concluded early in 1755. This settled, the Trustees' next task was to appoint staff to run the new museum. Interest from the funding provided by the lottery was only £1320 a year, so the staff would have to be few in number and poorly paid. Nonetheless, men of distinction were persuaded to take the vacant places. The establishment consisted of a Principal Librarian at the head, three Under-Librarians, each with an assistant, a porter (who absconded soon after his appointment), four maids and a messenger. The collections that comprised the British Museum were divided into the three "departments" of Printed Books, Manuscripts, and Natural and Artificial Productions, each one being the responsibility of one of the three Under-Librarians.

Specimens for public display were placed on the upper floors of Montagu House, reached via the main staircase. Duplicate specimens were stored below.

The collections in the Manor House in Chelsea were inspected and moved up to Bloomsbury, one hopes more carefully than they were moved out there nearly fifteen years earlier, and by the end of 1756 the keys of that house had been handed back to Sloane's heirs. There was a great deal to do in the new building. The roof had to be repaired, the whole house had to be cleaned and redecorated, bookcases and showcases had to be built, and the gardens laid out. Dr Gowin Knight, the Principal Librarian, drew up a scheme for the proper display of the natural history collections,

which would clearly be the main draw for the public. Considering the material to hand, he stated that "the fossils are the most simple, and therefore may properly be disposed in the first rank: next to them the vegetables; and lastly the animal substances. By this arrangement the Spectator will be gradually conducted from the simplest to the most compound and most perfect of nature's productions". In all it was four years before the public were finally allowed in to see their new museum, by resolution of the Trustees "That the museum be opened on Monday the fifteenth of January 1759".

Even then it was not easy to get inside. First "such studious and curious persons as are desirous to see the Museum" had to apply in writing to the porter, come back a day or two later to collect a ticket (assuming that they were judged to be "fit and proper persons"), and come back a third time on the day appointed for their visit. Visitors were taken round in groups of five, spending no more than one hour in each of the three departments. One must sympathize with one baffled visitor who wrote: "so rapid a passage through a vast suite of rooms in little more than one hour of time, with opportunities to cast but one poor longing look of astonishment on all the vast treasures of nature, antiquity, and literature, in the examination of which one might profitably spend years, confuses, stuns, and overpowers the visitor".

There was much to delight the naturalist in this great curiosity shop. The Entrance Hall contained basalt columns from the Giant's Causeway, slabs of serpentine and the skeleton of the unicorn fish to whet the visitor's appetite. At the top of the principal staircase the visitor entered a room containing Sloane's agates, jaspers, crystals, marbles, ores and gems. A second room contained fossil shells, bones, teeth, earths, petrifactions and incrustations, together with a display of modern shells that, it was thought, might "particularly claim the attention of the ladies". The third room, "no less curious and deserving of notice", contained fruits, aromatic woods and all manner of other vegetable productions, together with corals, whose nature was still somewhat uncertain, and insects, whose "history is very amusing and entertaining". A final natural history room was stocked with more insects, stuffed reptiles, birds and mammals of all kinds, "a great number and variety of articles preserved in spirits", and "a great variety of horns of different animals". There were of course no tea rooms, no toilets and no shop.

. . . .
The Entrance Hall of Montagu House, 1845.

The British Museum quickly began to attract gifts, all carefully recorded in "the large vellum book of benefactions" kept for the purpose. To take only a few examples, Gustavus Brander, a Swedish merchant, presented a number of collections of minerals and fossils from the south of England from 1756; Sir William Hamilton sent lavas, breccias and bombs from Vesuvius and Mount Etna in the years from 1768; and the Royal Society gave their extensive but miscellaneous collection of rarities in 1781. Altogether 250 donors added thousands specimens to the natural history collections during the first twenty years of its existence. As the collection grew it became more difficult to find things, and the need for catalogues became obvious. Sloane's own catalogues

Banksia serrata, *one of many new species collected by Banks and Solander during their voyage on the* Endeavour. *Sketches with coloured details were made on the voyage by Sydney Parkinson and later used as the basis for paintings completed by other artists.*

were described as being "well writ", but were not well organized, and the Trustees were delighted to appoint the distinguished young Swede Daniel Solander to produce a series of "systematical catalogues", giving the names, synonyms, locality and use of the different objects in the natural history collection. The Trustees, perhaps used to cataloguing books in a library, had no idea how difficult this would be. Solander was faced with trying to name thousands of unidentified objects, using only a few books by Linnaeus and others as a source. He did produce a vast number of paper slips, each describing and discussing a particular animal or plant. These slips, now bound as fifty-one small volumes and preserved in the Library, constitute a formidable store of data, but they were not at all the sort of neatly tabulated catalogue that the Trustees had in mind. The one thing Solander did complete and publish was a catalogue of the Hampshire fossils presented to the British Museum by Gustavus Brander.

In 1768 Solander was given leave of absence to sail around the world with Captain James Cook and Joseph Banks on board the *Endeavour*. The ship returned to England in 1771, loaded with natural history treasures, and it was soon after Solander's return to the British Museum in 1773 that collections gathered on the voyage began to arrive as gifts from Cook himself and others. They were featured in a South Sea Room in Montagu House, and many remain among The Natural History Museum's greatest treasures. Solander died in 1782 before he could accomplish much more. Joseph (later Sir Joseph) Banks, on the other hand, lived a long life, and became a great power in British science and natural history. He was a Trustee of the British Museum for forty years, and encouraged many important donations and purchases. His statue still stands on the Botany Landing of The Natural History Museum. However, he hindered the British Museum in some ways, and his own house and collections, rather than the museum, became the national centre for botany. Not until Banks' death in 1820, and the transfer of his collections and curator to the British Museum, did botany make any real progress there.

. . . .
For almost fifty years, Sir Joseph Banks' library and botanical collections at Soho Square easily rivalled those at the British Museum as a magnet for botanists.

The truth was, as Banks must have realized, that things were pretty dismal at the British Museum. For most of its first fifty years the staff seem to have done little more than take parties of visitors around the galleries, deal with the occasional gifts that arrived, and argue among themselves on minor points of protocol and precedence. Admission remained a tortuous procedure, and visitor numbers stayed under 10,000 a year throughout the 18th century. It could not even produce its own guidebook, though various commercial booksellers were happy to oblige. Charles Morton, Principal Librarian from 1776 until 1799, was easy-going and happy enough to let things drift, but unwilling or incapable of taking any initiative. He disgraced himself with the Trustees by remaining on leave when the British Museum was threatened with attack during the Gordon riots of 1780 and troops swarmed all over the gardens. Edward Whitaker Gray, who took charge of the natural history collections after the death of Solander, was little better, being appointed more for his social graces than for his knowledge of the subject. The British Museum was certainly kept very short of money, but this in itself is no excuse for its sluggish progress.

....

The Rosetta Stone, which provided the key to Egyptian hieroglyphs, was just one of many treasures acquired by the British Museum in the late 17th and early 18th centuries.

In spite of this, collections of antiquities did begin to pour in. First came the vases and other Italian antiquities of Sir William Hamilton, purchased for £8410 in 1772; Egyptian treasures confiscated from the French, including the Rosetta Stone, arrived in 1802; the huge collection of Roman classical sculptures formed by Charles Towneley was bought for £20,000 in 1805; and finally the Elgin Marbles from the Parthenon were acquired for £35,000 in 1816. It is not surprising that in 1807 antiquities were set up as a separate department, leaving natural history as part of the new "Department of Natural History and Modern Curiosities". Montagu House was quite unable to cope with this influx, and a new building appeared on the Trustees' agenda for the first time. A number of splendid collections of minerals were purchased during the same period, starting with Charles Hatchett's collection in 1799, and culminating in the purchase of the minerals collected by Charles Greville, nephew of Sir William Hamilton, for £13,727 in 1810. By 1815 the mineral saloon was one of the highlights of Montagu House, and the earliest editions of the official guidebook devoted forty-four pages to minerals and twelve pages to the whole of the rest of natural history. With these acquisitions the British Museum began to change from "a place where obscure natural curiosities may be seen", to the home of fine, comprehensive and scientific collections.

A number of more active and enlightened staff were appointed at this period, though more by accident than design. Dr George Shaw, for example, joined as assistant to Edward Whitaker Gray in 1791. He was a writer and a popularizer, committed to what the 20th century was to call "the public understanding of science". Soon after joining, Shaw applied to the Trustees for permission to give lectures, but was turned down with a rebuke. A year or two later he was reprimanded for allowing a surgeon and a draughts-man to see the collections without permission, and all in all was guilty of "sundry transgressions of duty", most of which would seem perfectly normal practice today. He was responsible for a great clear-out of duplicate and decayed specimens in 1808 and 1809, which led to many of Sloane's stuffed specimens being burnt in a series of huge bonfires out in the British Museum gardens, and then to the transfer of a large number of medical and anatomical specimens to the Royal College of Surgeons. Shaw was certainly not a model museum curator, indeed his successor found the collections in a "deplorable state", but he certainly did try to make use of material in the collections for the benefit of the public. Another even brighter spark was William Elford Leach, who was appointed assistant in Natural History in 1814, after the death of Shaw. Leach was quite different from his predecessors in that he actively tried to build up the zoology collections, rather than just sitting to wait for things to arrive. He had an international perspective on his science, having visited Paris and met the great Baron Georges Cuvier. He acquired specimens for the British Museum on his visit and sent duplicates to France in exchange. Leach was off collecting again in 1816 when he "requested permission to visit the British Islands and such parts of the coast as produce peculiar specimens of zoology". In another innovative move, Leach supplied William Swainson with a stock of glass bottles to encourage him to collect in Brazil, an investment that paid off handsomely when 800 insects were received. He also used the collections as the basis of his own researches, publishing twenty books and papers on insects, crustaceans and molluscs during his seven years at the British Museum. Leach left on sick leave in the summer of 1820 and never returned.

(opposite)
George Shaw,
museum curator,
encouraged
the access of the
public to the
Museum's
collections.

The collections
themselves were
beset with prob-
lems. Damage
like this, caused
by beetles, meant
they were being
literally eaten
away.

The rumblings of discontent at the state of the British Museum came to a head in 1823 when John George Children, an assistant in the Department of Antiquities, was appointed to succeed Leach in the Department of Natural History. English naturalists were furious. Just when zoology at least had made some progress at the British Museum, here was a man appointed who knew nothing at all of zoology or botany, although just a little mineral chemistry. Worse still, he had been appointed over the head of a well-known and respected young zoologist, William Swainson. Swainson's supporters mobilized, and one of them wrote an expose of the British Museum in the *Edinburgh Review*. All was revealed. The dreary and disordered state of the public galleries, still only visited by a few thousand visitors a year; the terrible condition of collections behind the scenes, ravaged by moths, beetles and moulds; the complete lack of interest in or understanding of science displayed by members of the Board of Trustees; and finally the system of patronage that led to the appointment of unqualified and unmotivated staff to positions of key importance in the scientific life of the country. It was a damning and very well publicized report on what the great Sir Humphry Davy had described as "this ancient, misapplied and, one might say, useless Museum".

Montagu House, some sixty years
after it opened was in a parlous state,
badly managed and attracting few
visitors to the dull and chaotic exhibits.

All this gave the British Museum unwelcome publicity, but did lead eventually to the appointment of a Select Committee of the House of Commons "to enquire into the condition, management and affairs of the British Museum". Members of this committee were nothing if not thorough. Through the summer of 1835 they interviewed staff, from the Principal Librarian downwards, and the following year they spoke to a wide range of scientists, naturalists and other scholars. Eighteen recommendations, together with complete transcripts of the interviews, were published late in 1836, and still make fascinating reading. We can read the words of the most senior staff, Sir Henry Ellis and the Revd Josiah Forshall, as they attempt to defend the status quo, and to show, for example, the dangers of allowing the lower orders into the galleries. Charles Konig, the Keeper of Natural History, and John George Children come across as well-intentioned and hard-working, but lacking initiative and any real grasp of their subjects, and the outside experts were eager to criticize and put forward their own pet schemes. The most extraordinary contributions came from John Edward Gray, who was a temporary assistant working on the zoological collections, and whose knowledge of the British Museum and its work, as well as of the latest developments in zoology both at home and abroad, put his superiors to shame. As will be seen, Gray was to play a large part in transforming the British Museum over the next thirty years.

The eighteen resolutions that make up the Committee's final report were disappointingly flimsy. The Board of Trustees survived unchanged, better consultation among senior staff and between them and the Trustees was called for, the Department of Natural History was to be subdivided, and catalogues and accession registers were required for all collections. But the Committee bent over backwards to avoid any hint of criticism against either trustees or staff, "whose talents, good conduct, and general and scientific acquirements, are universally admitted".

However, for the British Museum, there could be no going back. It would take another thirty years to undo the harm done to its reputation by the mistakes of the past, but a course for the future was set.

A Great Sea Dragon

It was purchased by the British Museum from one Thomas Hawkins (1810–1889), the eccentric and flamboyant son of a Somersetshire farmer. Hawkins collected furiously from the Lias of Street and Glastonbury, moving tons of rock where necessary, developing his specimens and giving them fancy names. He also bought specimens (including the giant ichthyosaur) from the celebrated fossil collector Mary Anning and other dealers. In 1833 (aged only 23!) he tried to sell a large collection of fossils to the British Museum for the huge sum of £4,000. It was turned down by the Trustees but, undaunted, he published a grandiose "coffee-table" description of the specimens entitled *Memoirs of Ichthyosauri and Plesiosauri,* and renewed his offer the following year. William Buckland, the famous Oxford geologist, smoothed the way, providing his own valuation of the collection (a mere £1,310). He also wrote to or spoke to bishops,

The largest of Hawkins' sea dragons, Temno-dontosaurus platydon, *is 194-203 million years old.*

lords, a duke and an archbishop to ensure that the purchase was approved by both the Trustees and by Parliament. There were no problems this time round, and in the autumn of 1834 Hawkins' fossils were delivered to the British Museum.

It was then that the trouble began. Had the British Museum got what it paid for? Had the specimens been tampered with? Was the price too high? Alarmingly, a collection that should have added much-needed prestige to the fossil collection rapidly turned into a public relations disaster. When Charles Konig

(Keeper of Geology) had a good look at the fossils he was horrified to discover that the largest ichthyosaur was "made up and all over restored with plaster of Paris and altogether unfit to be exhibited to the public without derogation from the character of the British Museum". Konig proposed that the plaster bits should be scraped off, painted a different colour, or referred to in both the label and the Museum guide. Anyone looking at this magnificent specimen, one of the most complete of its kind, might well conclude that he was grossly overreacting. Konig had calmed down by Easter, but by then the damage had been done. *The Times*, the *Literary Gazette* and the *Athenaeum* all covered the story with glee, and word got around that the British Museum had been taken for a ride. The Parliamentary Committee investigating the museum in 1835 made a meal of the Hawkins affair, devoting twenty pages of their final report to it.

Whatever the anguish caused at the time, Hawkins' fossil reptiles are among The Natural History Museum's most popular exhibits, and twenty-six of his specimens are still on display there.

. . . .
Frontispiece of Thomas Hawkins' The Book of the Great Sea Dragons.

CHAPTER : 3

A NEW BUILDING:
THE BLOOMSBURY DEVELOPMENT

The British Museum took many years to recover from the hammering it received at the hands of the Parliamentary Commission of 1835, but recover it did. The process was helped by its magnificent new buildings, by the improved calibre of its staff, and by the slow increase in the money made available by Parliament.

Some sixty years after opening, Montagu House was crowded and crumbling. Each of those years had seen large sums spent on patching up the decaying structure, and at one time things had got so bad that the Trustees considered evacuating it altogether. A Building Committee was set up as early as 1802, recommending expansion into the gardens to the north of Montagu House. The first stage of this expansion was the small but elegant new wing built for the Townley and other collections of antiquities in 1808. Purchase of the Elgin and Phigalian Marbles in 1815–1816 led to another space crisis, temporarily solved by construction of a wood and brick shed just west of the Townley Gallery. Clearly, the time for full-scale rebuilding could not be long delayed. It was the presentation by King George IV of the library formed by his father George III that finally settled the matter. This magnificent bequest of over 60,000 books came on condition that "a separate room should be appropriated for its reception", and such a room did not exist in Montagu House.

Robert Smirke of the Office of Works was the architect entrusted with rebuilding the British Museum. Smirke had built Gothic castles at Lowther and Eastnor, and Tudor mansions at Wilton and Drayton Manor, but his real love was the Greek Revival, and it was a great Greek 'temple of the arts' that slowly emerged in Bloomsbury. The quadrangular plan was presented to Parliament and given the go-ahead in 1823, and the east wing was completed in 1827 to house the King's Library. Work proceeded steadily

Montagu House became increasingly delapidated and was finally demolished in 1850. It had housed the Museum's collections for 85 years.

through the 1830s, and speeded up in 1840 when Sir Robert Peel persuaded the Treasury to increase the rate of spending. By the time Robert Smirke retired in 1846, his brother Sydney was only left to supervise completion of the forecourt and lodges and sundry small galleries.

Natural history displays eventually occupied the first floor of the south, east and north wings, roughly one-third of the British Museum's floor space, and a great deal more than in the old building. The minerals moved into the new building in 1829, followed by fossils, shells and the British birds, and the eastern galleries were opened to the public in 1831. The second phase of the move came in 1840 and 1841, when mammals, reptiles, fish and animals in spirits were moved from Montagu House into the north wing, and the old building was demolished a few years later with, apparently, few regrets. The British Museum now looked from the outside like an institution for a great nation to be proud of.

. . . .
Robert Smirke's new building for the British Museum reflected his love of the Greek Revival.

We have seen how Sir Joseph Banks' lack of confidence in the British Museum led to him making his own house a national centre for botany, at the expense of the museum. In his will, Banks left his library and herbarium to Robert Brown, the distinguished botanist and traveller who had acted as his librarian and curator for ten years, but with the proviso that at Brown's death or earlier they were to become the property of the British Museum. By 1827, with the new building making good progress, the Trustees began to negotiate with Brown for the transfer. It was agreed that Brown would join the staff as Keeper of the Banksian Botanical Collections,

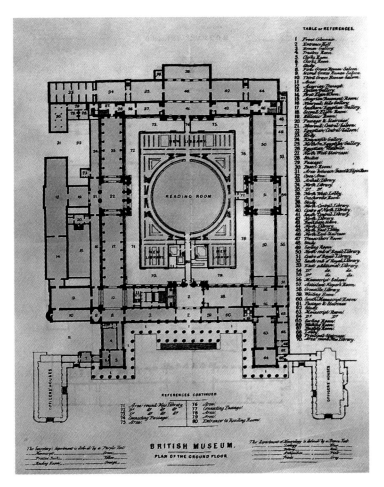

TABLE of REFERENCES.

REFERENCES CONTINUED.

BRITISH MUSEUM.
PLAN OF THE GROUND FLOOR.

....
Plan of the British Museum building in Bloomsbury, which was to replace Montagu House. Seventy separate areas are marked, almost all devoted to the collections, and grouped around the great dome of the Reading Room.

at a rank and salary equal to the other keepers, but working only two days a week. He would be responsible for Sir Joseph's herbarium, and his valuable collection of botanical manuscripts, drawings and copperplates. The printed books were unfortunately passed to the Department of Printed Books, a move that would be a source of intermittent friction for the next hundred years. The position of botany was not yet secure, however. The Sloane Herbarium and other botanical collections remained under Charles Konig, Keeper of Natural History, and no guarantee was given that Brown would be replaced should he die or retire. Not until 1834 did the Trustees agree that all the botanical collections should come under Brown, and only in 1837 was Botany accepted as one of the three branches of the Department of Natural History, albeit the smallest and least prestigious.

A new threat emerged in 1848, when Brown was interviewed by the Parliamentary Commissioners. The question was posed: would it be advantageous if your collections could be united with a good botanical garden? In other words, how about transferring the Botanical Branch from the British Museum to Kew Gardens? The question was raised more forcibly in 1860, after Brown's death, when a Parliamentary Committee was set up, and many London botanists argued forcibly in favour of the move. It all came to nothing when it was admitted that Kew did not have the space, the staff or the funds to take on the extra responsibility. Eleven years later the whole matter was aired again, but by that time the able and dynamic William Carruthers was in charge of the Department, and it was easy to demonstrate that botany at the British Museum was distinct and different from that at Kew. There, for the time being, the matter rested. Relations with Kew Gardens took many years to recover, reaching a low point in 1875 when representatives of the British Museum and Kew argued in court over the ownership of the great collections of Angolan plants amassed for the King of Portugal by Friedrich Welwitsch in the 1850s.

Of the members of staff interviewed by the 1835 Parliamentary Commission, one stood above the rest in enthusiasm, knowledge and breadth of vision: John Edward Gray. He had been working as a zoologist for ten years, although he had no formal appointment. His talents were recognized both in and out of the British

Museum, and when John George Children retired in 1840 Gray succeeded him as Keeper of the Zoological Branch of the Natural History Department, supported by zoologists throughout Europe. Gray was never in any doubt about what the British Museum should become. He wanted his department to house the finest and most complete collection of zoological specimens that it was possible to gather, backed by the best library. He wanted staff and associate workers who could curate and research the collections to produce detailed catalogues. He wanted a stream of distinguished visiting scientists who would use the collections to advance scientific knowledge, and he wanted exhibition galleries that would spread a knowledge and love of zoology among the public. In 1840 there was a very long way to go.

The move into the new buildings in 1840 and 1841 gave Gray space for expansion, of which he took full advantage. For several years Gray was tireless in using his network of contacts to encourage gifts and sales to the British Museum. In the first five years of his keepership annual accessions of mammals rose from about one hundred to over a thousand, of birds from three hundred to over two thousand. Among the collections that came in during these years were the first of John Gould's Australian collections, mammals and birds from the Cape of Good Hope presented by the Earl of Derby, mammals and birds of Nepal from Brian H. Hodgson, and Antarctic mammals, birds, reptiles and fish from the voyage of the *Erebus* and *Terror* under Captain Ross. At this rate, even the great new building would soon be full.

Gray was keen to extend the scope of his branch wherever he could. Until 1845 the zoological collections consisted only of skins and stuffed specimens, bones being the preserve of the Royal College of Surgeons in

Lincoln's Inn Fields. Gray found a way of getting round this when Brian H. Hodgson, the British Resident in Nepal, offered his immensely valuable collection of mammalian and other skins and skeletons to the British Museum with the condition (suggested by Gray) that all must be kept together. In spite of protests from the Surgeons, the Trustees were not prepared to risk losing the whole lot, and osteology became an accepted part of the work of the Zoology Branch. Gray was less successful in a second piece of empire-building. He believed that fossil and living organisms were best studied and exhibited together, whereas in the British Museum fossils were the responsibility of the Mineralogical Branch, whose head was the ageing Charles Konig. In spite of persuading the British Association to petition the Trustees on the subject in 1840, nothing was done, and the following year Gray literally highjacked William Gilbertson's collection of Carboniferous Limestone fossils for his own department. Not until 1857 did the formation of the Department of Geology settle the question, and thereafter fossils were studied quite separately from their living relatives.

Gray was not only a notable scientist, he was also a dedicated curator, convinced of the value of both registers and catalogues. The system of registering specimens as they arrived started in 1837 as a result of a recommendation made by the 1835 Parliamentary Commissioners. Several of the earliest zoological registers are in Gray's own handwriting, and his annual reports always proudly record that incoming collections have been duly registered. These volumes were invaluable for keeping track of specimens within the British Museum. His other enthusiasm was for catalogues, in which all the specimens of a particular group of animals were described. Catalogues of a large number of zoological groups were published during the 1840s and 1850s, and sold and were used all over the world. No fewer than twenty were by Gray himself, while others were prepared by members of his staff and by outside specialists.

These gains were made in the face of almost insuperable odds, for working conditions at the British Museum were wretched. The offices, such as they were, were dark, dirty and overcrowded.

Russels Indian serpents. Part. 1.

1. Boa lineata Shaw   Bungarus fasciatus (Ther. 137/1806)
2. Boa Horratta St.   Echis carinata Mer. J Wagler
3. Boa fasciata St.   Bungarus annularis Mer. Boa aspida Wigh
4. Boa Viperina St. Python. Gongylophis Wagler
5. Col. Naia,   Naia tripudians Boie
6. ,, —"—   —+— ——— + Mer
7.   Echydra, elegans/Mer 153/
8.   Elaps innaculata Mer 163 . Wagler
9.   Cophias viridis 15 Mer Boa
10.   Natrix stolatus 17 Mer
11.   —+— —+— 117 Mer
12.   Dryinus nasutus Mer 136/ D oxyrhynchus Bel
                        Dryophis nasutus Boa 11
13.   Dryophis Passericki Mer. D Russellianus Bell
14.   Natrix Linnaeorum 25 Mer
15.   Homalopsis Java Boa Mer.175.
16.   Malignus 24 Mer
17. Hydruscanereus St. Python rhynchops Mer.
18.   Natrix d. cerus . 110 Mer.

Part of John Edward Gray's handwritten register of reptiles and amphibia. This part deals with Indian snakes collected by Russel.

The Nepalese collections of mammals and birds by Brian H. Hodgson were one of the valuable acquisitions made by John Edward Gray.

The only room where visiting scientists could work was the Insect Room, deep in the basement, where maybe four or five would have to crowd in together. It was described as "quite unfit for students" in 1860, and it is not surprising that some, such as Dr Andrew Smith, the authority on South African natural history, refused to work at the British Museum at all. Salaries were small, with no provision for any pension, and ill-health was common, with breakdowns and even suicide being not unknown. In 1848 Dr William Baird, who worked on the huge collection of molluscs, petitioned Gray that having worked for seven years, he was paid only fourteen shillings a day "for each day actually worked", which was sufficient for only the bare necessities of life. Within the Department there was only enough money for the most basic furniture and equipment. These conditions were made to seem

Once the British Museum was open to a wider public the natural history galleries proved much more popular than those containing antiquities

NATURE'S TREASUREHOUSE

worse by a petty and humiliating bureaucracy imposed from above. Departmental archives for this period are full of peremptory memoranda signed by the Principal Librarian or his office staff, relating to the infringements of regulations concerning purchases, exchanges, leave and the like. Gray was not the only keeper to suffer in this way: Nevil Story-Maskelyne, Keeper of Mineralogy, received the following letter from the Principal Librarian in March 1858: "Dear Sir, with reference to my letter to you of the 2nd instant and your answer thereto, I am directed by the Trustees to call your attention to the fifteenth rule Chap. III of the Statutes and to acquaint you that the Standing Committee observing that this rule has not been complied uniformly with, have instructed me to express their desire that it should in future be strictly observed".

The fact was that science and natural history were held in low esteem by the Principal Librarian and most of the Trustees. Konig pointed out to the Parliamentary Commissioners of 1850 that, although natural history was the original strength and raison d'être of the British Museum, its place had now been usurped by the library and the antiquities departments. Of the fifty or so Trustees, eighteen made up a Standing Committee that did all the work, and of these the only two with any scientific attainments were one distinguished geologist (Sir Roderick Murchison) and a collector of fossil fish (Sir Phillip Egerton). There is no doubt that Antonio Panizzi, Principal Librarian from 1856, felt a great deal more comfortable in the company of classical scholars and antiquaries than alongside entomologists and palaeontologists, and would on any day "give three mammoths for an Aldus" (i.e. an early printed book). The question put to him by the 1860 Parliamentary Commission: "have you ever engaged in scientific investigation?" received a disdainful "never" in reply. Panizzi was clearly of the opinion that the natural history departments had best leave the British Museum altogether, and that it would be less smelly, and a quieter, more scholarly place as a result.

It must have irked the Principal Librarian and Trustees that the natural history galleries were enormously popular. By the middle of the century the British Museum authorities had lost that fear of the lower orders that so characterized the 1820s and 1830s. There had been a major scare in 1848 when the Chartists had marched on London, and muskets, cutlasses and pikes had been issued so that the staff could defend their collections. Although Antonio Panizzi in particular was spoiling for a fight, the day

. . . .
John Edward Gray was hugely instrumental in the expansion of the natural history collections. His bust is on the left of this picture taken of the Mammalion Saloon in 1875

passed quietly as the demonstrations fizzled out. As the old restrictions on entry were gradually removed, visitor numbers increased. Admission tickets had been abolished in 1805, and by 1810 "any person of decent appearance" was allowed to wander through the galleries as they wished, at least on Mondays, Wednesdays and Fridays, the remaining two days of the week being reserved for artists. The year 1851 was a time when the British Museum was truly crowded with visitors, with over two million of them up in town for the Great Exhibition. It was found that sailors and their girlfriends, bricklayers, housemaids and all manner of others were coming to the British Museum without ill effect, and that generally they preferred lions and tigers to statues and ceramics. Natural history as a whole had become enormously popular with the general public, and the British Museum was reaping the reward. Popular books and magazines were in print, local societies flourished, times were easier and more people had the leisure and money to travel up to London. Over a fortnight it was found that as many people were crowded into the natural history galleries as were to be found in the whole of the rest of the British Museum. The authorities accepted that the museum had a twin purpose: instruction for serious academic people, and rational amusement for the masses. It was felt that exposing the middle and working classes to a comprehensive display of the works of creation might improve their moral fibre and, also, make them proud to be British. "Gratify their curiosity and excite their wonder" became the twin aims of the British Museum.

What was there to see? A visitor in 1851, arriving at the Main Entrance and buying a copy of the densely printed *Synopsis of the British Museum* for one shilling, would have headed up the great staircase to start the tour. First came the three southern zoological rooms, containing stuffed antelopes, sheep and goats, elephants and rhinoceroses, apes and monkeys, "rapacious beasts", and, tucked almost out of sight on the case tops, the porpoises, dolphins and seals. Then, turning left at the southeast corner of the building, came the Eastern Zoological Gallery, which contained 166 wall-cases of birds, including the ever-popular remains of the dodo, and 49 table-cases of shells, as well as a display of a miscellaneous collection of painted portraits just below the high ceiling. A left turn brought the Northern Zoological Gallery into view, a series of smaller rooms containing reptiles, amphibians, fish, various invertebrates, and a room devoted to British animals. The energetic visitor could then move out into the North Gallery to view the

mineral collection, displayed in systematic order in sixty showcases, and including the meteorites, gold nuggets, rubies and
sapphires. Finally came the six rooms of fossils, in which were displayed the remains of ichthyosaurs and plesiosaurs, the mammoth
and the mastodon, as well as innumerable ammonites, trilobites
and other extinct monsters. There was certainly masses to see!

. . . .
Part of the
extensive display
of birds and shells
which enthralled
the mid-19th
century visitors.

The year 1856 was one of change for the British Museum.
First came the retirement of Sir Henry Ellis, who had been the
quiet and gentlemanly Principal Librarian since 1827, and the
appointment of the aforementioned forceful and dynamic Antonio
Panizzi to take his place, "to the delight of his many friends and
the baffled rage of his equally numerous enemies". This appointment filled those who worried about the state of science at the
museum with alarm, and the feeling grew that something must
be done about it. The British Museum had to have an imperator,
who would stand up and fight for science. Just the man was to
hand in the person of Richard Owen. Owen was one of the most
distinguished anatomists of his day, well known to the public for
his reconstructions of extinct animals and for coining the word
"dinosaur". He had had a successful career at the Royal College of

Surgeons, transforming a small medical museum into a great centre of comparative anatomy that rivalled the British Museum itself in some areas. But his talents were clearly not being used to the full, and he wanted a change. It was Lord Macaulay who pressed his case with his fellow Trustees, and Owen was duly appointed to the newly created post of Superintendent of the Natural History Departments in May 1856. At the same time the old Natural History Department ceased to exist, and its four branches of Botany, Geology, Mineralogy and Zoology became fully fledged departments, each with their own Keeper and with Richard Owen, the Superintendent, over all.

. . . .

Richard Owen
at the age of 40.
He is holding
the leg bone of
an extinct giant
moa.

While Owen's scientific reputation was second to none, he was not popular among his fellow scientists, being seen as vindictive and untrustworthy. News that he was coming to the British Museum must have been highly unwelcome. Panizzi needed to be reassured that his own position was still intact and that Owen would be his subsidiary. The heads of the natural history departments were determined that Owen would not interfere in the running of their departments, and that he should not stand in the way of what little contact they had with the Principal Librarian and Trustees. The truth was that in many ways this turned out to be a bad move for Owen. He received a rise in salary and an increase in prestige, but he sacrificed his old freedom of action. Owen, too, was now exposed to correction and reprimand by the bureaucrats. The exact job that he was supposed to do was not well defined, and at times he seemed equally at loggerheads with those below and above him.

Owen's outstanding contribution was to force the issue of shortage of space and to fight for a new and separate Museum of Natural History. Probably nobody else could have fought and won that battle, and The Natural History Museum in South Kensington owes its form and its very existence to Richard Owen.

The Reeves Drawings

As well as extensive holdings of books, journals and manuscripts, The Natural History Museum has an unparalleled collection of artwork. The Reeves drawings are one of many examples of the value of accurately observed and painstakingly executed illustrations.

The Reeves illustration of a slow loris.

John Reeves (1774–1856) was not a professional naturalist. An orphan from an early age, he rose from a job in the counting house of a London tea broker to the post of Inspector of Tea in England with the Honourable East India Company. This famous company was a powerful concern in eastern Asia and Reeves soon advanced to become its Chief Inspector of Tea in the Chinese trading port of Canton. There he apparently had plenty of time outside the tea season (September–March) to indulge an interest in local wildlife.

Reeves set about collecting all manner of animals, birds and fishes, which he sent to various institutes in England, including the British Museum and Chelsea Physic Garden. He was responsible for introducing many plants to Europe, and the decks of sailing ships leaving Canton often sported miniature greenhouses of Reeves' own design to protect plants on the voyage. However, it was not as a collector that Reeves was to make his greatest contribution to science.

In 1817, Reeves commissioned Chinese artists to produce four identical sets of illustrations under his supervision and some 2000 animals and plants were drawn in great detail from specimens. Also among the commissioned paintings are occasional examples of what are known as stock pictures. These are in a less formal style developed by Chinese painters at that time to satisfy the growing demand for local artwork from foreigners.

They were not drawn from life and were often composite illustrations not necessarily reflecting reality. For example, the leaves, flowers and fruit of entirely different plants might be depicted growing from the same stem. However, stock pictures were much appreciated by Reeves and some were obviously sufficiently accurate for them to be included in the sets.

Before Reeves' time few specimens had come out of China, mainly because of the severe restrictions on travel and other activities imposed on foreigners by the country's Manchu rulers. Little was known, therefore, of the plants and animals of the region and the Reeves drawings formed a major source of information. The quality of the paintings is such that scientists were able to describe eighty new species, mainly fish, despite the absence of specimens. Sir John Richardson, who owned one of the three sets of Reeves paintings now in The Natural History Museum, claimed that "These drawings are executed with a correctness and finish which will be sought for in vain in the older works on ichthyology, and which are not surpassed in the plates of any large European work of the present day". That claim, made in 1846, can be upheld even today.

. . . .
The Reeves illustration of a mango tree. The image is a compilation of flowering and fruiting shoots with young and mature leaves and is probably a stock picture.

CHAPTER 4

To South Kensington:
The great divide

Separation of the natural history departments from the rest of the
British Museum had been in the air for many years. The subject
had come up at the time of the 1835 Parliamentary Commission,
and was clearly not going to go away. There had even been talk of
piecemeal dispersal, with the fossils going to the Royal College of
Surgeons, the minerals to the Museum of Economic Geology and,
as we have seen, the plants going off to Kew. The facts were that
the collections were growing, the staff and the number of visiting
scientists were increasing, while the available space remained the
same. All the keepers complained about lack of space in their
departments, and none more forcibly than John Edward Gray in
Zoology. In a lurid report to the Trustees, Gray described how
the zoological collections had increased ten-fold since 1836 while
the space for their display had increased by a factor of only three.
He told of damp and crowded basement rooms, valuable and interesting specimens hidden away in drawers, and showcases so full
that specimens at the front hid those at the back. Larger specimens
were no longer accepted for the collection, as there was nowhere to
put them. Richard Owen knew of all this before he was appointed,
but none the less the scale of the problem must have come as a
shock to him: Gray was certainly not exaggerating. Owen's own
tiny and unheated room must have reminded him of the problem
every day. In a shrewd move he took a leading politician, William
Gladstone, on a comprehensive tour of the British Museum to
bring home the points he was making to the Trustees.

On the basis of reports from his keepers, Owen calculated
how much space would be needed for proper display of the
different classes of natural history object, and he drew up a plan
showing how these areas might be combined into a free-standing
natural history museum. The museum was to have two types of
display. The first, located in the centre, was to be devoted to typical
specimens of the different groups and was intended to serve the

*The Natural
History Museum
abounds with
terracotta
animals and
plants. The
eastern half of
the building
features extinct
species while
the western half
features living
ones including
this lion on the
exterior parapet.*

beginner in natural history as an introduction and index to the rest of the museum. Nearby was to be an exhibition of British natural history and also a lecture theatre, where members of the museum staff could explain their various specialities. There was even the idea that this area might be lit by gas and opened in the evenings for the benefit of working men who could not get to the museum during the day. Leading off this central area were a much larger series of departmental galleries, each devoted to a particular group of animals, to plants, minerals and fossils. A much higher level of previous knowledge was assumed in these areas, and visitors would be encouraged to study in depth rather than just wander around. His planning completed, Owen then announced to the Trustees that the time had come to divide the British Museum in two, separating the works of Man (books, manuscripts and antiquities) from the works of God (natural history). Perhaps to his surprise, the Trustees agreed with him in January 1860, albeit by a majority of only nine to eight, only seventeen of the British Museum's fifty Trustees having taken the trouble to attend the meeting.

. . . .

(opposite)
Thomas Huxley
as depicted in
the January 1871
issue of
Vanity Fair.

. . . .

Owen had strong
views on which
collections should
be displayed. This
sketch, made by
him in 1859, and
entitled "Idea of
a Museum of
Natural History",
shows the layout
of galleries for
different subjects.

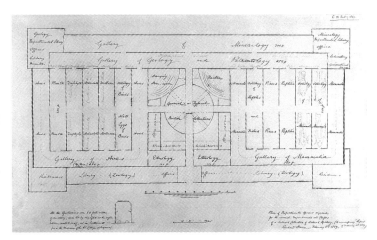

The next question was where to go? Could enough space be found close to the existing British Museum in Bloomsbury, or might South Kensington be a better option? The subject was hotly debated both inside and outside. A large number of "the promoters and cultivators of natural knowledge" petitioned the Government that natural history must stay in Bloomsbury, partly to benefit from the British Museum's library, but also for the sake of "the most intelligent of the working classes" who would not wish to travel all the way from (say) Bermondsey to South Kensington, then of course right on the western edge of London. Owen replied that he loved Bloomsbury, but that he loved ten acres more, meaning that he didn't care where natural history ended up, as long as it got lots of space. There was certainly space in South Kensington. The area was earmarked as a centre for science and the arts, following the work of Prince Albert and the success of the Great Exhibition of 1851. A large piece of land on the southern edge, which had been used for an International Exhibition, was about the right size, although currently occupied by the exhibition building, a great temporary shed, described as "one of the ugliest public buildings that was ever raised in this country" by the newspapers.

A row now blew up in the scientific world that went right to the heart of the purpose of the museum. On one side of the argument was Richard Owen, who believed that Britain, being the most powerful nation in the world, must have the biggest and best museum, and that the British public had a right to see comprehensive displays of all the species making up the natural world. He believed that the museum must be a faithful epitome of the natural world, whose purpose was, at least in part, to demonstrate the power and goodness of God. He was particularly concerned that there should be space for an adequate display of whales, both stuffed and as skeletons. This was why his sketch plan was for a building of 500,000 square feet (over 45,000 m^2) occupying a 10 acre (4 ha) site. On the other side was Thomas Huxley, famous as the friend and supporter of Charles Darwin, who believed that it was the scientist's responsibility to select specimens for display in the public galleries, leaving the vast bulk in storage, where they could be studied by specialists as required. Huxley wanted only a relatively small public museum, with storage in a separate building and even in a separate part of London. Owen was ridiculed in the press and in the House of Commons – did he really want to put all the different types of beetles out on display, wouldn't this fatigue and confuse the visitor? But nonetheless it was Owen's vision, rather than Huxley's, that won the day.

Clearing the South Kensington site involved demolishing the International Exhibition building, "one of the ugliest public buildings" in Britain.

By 1864, in spite of several setbacks, the Government had bought the International Exhibition site and demolished the building standing on it. A competition had been held that attracted twenty-one entrants and, after keen debate, the panel of judges had announced an engineer named Captain Francis Fowke as the winner. This was indeed a surprising choice, as it was Fowke who had been responsible for the much-reviled exhibition building that had only just been demolished. However, Fowke was given no chance to prove himself, dying before the year had ended. In a second surprising move, the Office of Works now appointed Alfred Waterhouse, a young and little-known Quaker architect from the north of England, who had not even entered the competition, to build the museum using Fowke's plans as a basis. It was 1868 before Waterhouse was ready to submit his own plans and, although they differed from Fowke's in many ways, they were warmly endorsed by the Trustees. The most crucial change was in architectural style. Fowke had produced an Italian Renaissance design, while Waterhouse wanted to build in a round-arched, Romanesque style. Although loosely based on a series of German churches and cathedrals that he had seen on his travels, the new Natural History Museum was no slavish copy of any existing building. There are Waterhousian elements that are found in no genuine Romanesque building, such as the great staircase in the Central Hall, the dormer windows of the main façade, and the traceried windows of the galleries. This style, together with the terracotta he used as the building's facing, allowed Waterhouse to decorate the building with natural history motifs. He and Richard Owen worked together to come up with designs for a whole menagerie of animals, both living and extinct, and a botanic garden full of plants. These figures were more than just decoration, being meant to reinforce the education aspects of the gallery displays, and so extinct animals and plants are to be found in the eastern galleries where the rocks and fossils were on show, and living animals in the western, zoological galleries. Educational or not, they have delighted visitors ever since.

At the end of 1868, with work about to start in South Kensington, the whole thing was put up in the air again when the Commissioner of Works suggested that it might be better to use a site on the Embankment, opposite what is now the Royal Festival Hall. A Parliamentary Select Committee was set up to look into the matter, and among those called to give evidence was Thomas Huxley. He was clearly in good form, giving evidence that the

Embankment was a better site from the point of view of working-class visitors, and quoting an artisan who had declared that the museum "might as well be in New Zealand as South Kensington for our purpose, because we cannot get there". He then attacked once again the whole basis of Owen's museum, proposing that alternate galleries should be devoted to public display and to study, thereby halving the amount of material on show, and providing ample space for visiting scientists. He envisaged scientists being able to open the back of the public gallery wall-cases to remove specimens for study. There was support for his views on the Committee, and Owen must have been relieved that a new Commissioner of Works slashed the budget in 1870, ending any hope of a riverside museum.

Back in South Kensington the foundation stone of the new museum was laid in 1873, and construction went ahead through

. . . .
Alfred Waterhouse was only 36 when he was offered the chance to build the new mueusm in South Kensington. The project occupied the next 14 years of his life.

the 1870s. Waterhouse had terrible problems trying to cut his costs from the original budget of £500,000 to the miserable £330,000, which was all that the new Commissioner would allow him. His solution was to build in two parts. The first part, comprising the south front and the core, was to be built straight away, with the east, west and north galleries being built as and when funds became available. Quite predictably, funds never did become available, or at least not until the 1960s and 1970s, by which time Romanesque wings were quite out of the question. Waterhouse also had to cut corners on the internal decoration, replacing wooden ceilings with plaster ones, and generally lowering the specification. Most visitors today, looking at the lovely painted ceilings, the wrought iron and the mosaic floors, feel that London got good value for money in the end. The building was complete in the middle of 1880, and the departments of Mineralogy and Geology were the first to move across from Bloomsbury.

Easter Monday, 18th April 1881, was the opening day; "a great day with the young people of the Metropolis" wrote the author of the first leader in *The Times*. Forty thousand visitors were admitted during the first two weeks that the British Museum (Natural History) as it was officially named, was open. Once they had

A drawing by Waterhouse of the interior of his Romanesque design and showing the abundant carvings and intricate details he intended to use. Waterhouse added his name over the lower left archway.

The Central Hall in 1882, still devoid of exhibits one year after The Natural History Museum opened in South Kensington.

negotiated the steps, and handed in their sticks and umbrellas (a rather curious security measure), they were free to explore the vast building, with its mile or so (over 1.5 km) of wall space and 4 acres (1.6 ha) of flooring. There was not a great deal to see to begin with. The fossil galleries on the eastern ground floor attracted a lot of attention, with a reporter to the *Saturday Review* enthusing that "there are few objects so exciting to the imagination as these colossal fragments of antediluvian life".

The main entrance to The Natural History Museum in South Kensington in November 1881, six months after it opened to the public.

However, the same writer considered that the Mineral Gallery was "not particularly exhilarating" and that the botanical collections, while ready for students, were still too confused for the general public. The rest of the Museum was empty – the Bird Gallery was so empty that "even a sparrow would attract attention", and it would be two more years until everything was complete. Still, the general opinion was that the Museum was a great success, and that once the "stuffed wild beasts" were moved over from Bloomsbury it would become a place well worth visiting. Certainly Waterhouse's new building made the old Bloomsbury displays seem "dull, close, crowded and fatiguing".

An editorial in the scientific journal *Nature* the following month was, as one might expect, more critical. While admitting that the building was very impressive, the elaborate and ornate internal decoration was condemned as "a serious mistake", which would impede the layout of displays. The semi-sacred style of the Central Hall was likewise dismissed as "mistaken", and the writer predicted a perpetual conflict between the views of the keepers of collections and the architects who built homes for them. The exhibitions in the galleries were described as "entirely praise-worthy", with the provision of maps and diagrams and explanatory text being such an advance over the dry old labelling back at Bloomsbury. Best of all, the writer welcomed the popular guide-books which, on sale at one penny each, and "replete with most valuable information", made the displays accessible to all.

This was truly Owen's museum. He had fought since 1859 for a national museum of natural history, and now one had opened. Many of its features derived directly from Owen's own view of the natural world, which, particularly in his rejection of Darwinian evolution, seemed hopelessly out of date by the end of the century. But even his fiercest critics could not deny his achievement. Owen remained in post as Superintendent of the Natural History Departments until the end of 1883 when, aged 79, he retired.

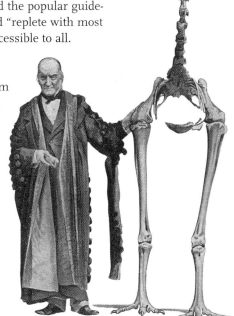

Richard Owen, aged c. 73, with the skeleton of a giant moa. The photograph recreates the portrait of Owen holding the leg bone of this bird painted 33 years earlier.

COFFEA·ARABICA   NICOTIANA·TABACVM   GOSSYPIVM·BARBADENSE

....
Three of the ceiling panels above the stairs at the south end of the Central Hall. The plants are (left to right) coffee, tobacco and cotton.

Alfred Waterhouse adorned his building with copious ornamentation, from columns representing the trunks of fossil plants to weather vanes in the form of fishes. Inside and out, the terracotta facing abounds with animals, birds, fishes, leaves and flowers. Perhaps the single most spectacular area is the ceiling of the Central Hall of the Museum. This is made up of a series of painted panels, 162 in total, divided into eighteen sets of nine panels. They were painted by the firm of Messrs Best and Lea, of Manchester, but otherwise little is now known about their design. However, an article in *The British Architect and Northern Engineer* from June 1878 gives some idea of the underlying concept. "The lower panels will have representations of foliage treated conventionally. The upper panels will be treated with more variety of colour and the designs will be of an archaic character. The chief idea to be represented is that of growth. The colours will be arranged so that the most brilliant will be near the apex of the roof". If these were indeed Waterhouse's aims, they were certainly achieved. There is a further clue to the thinking behind the selection of species depicted. Almost all are plants of economic importance at the time, providing a variety of foods, timber, clothing and medicines. Of the forty-eight species depicted, only three, *Banksia speciosa, Magnolia auriculata* and *Rhododendron formosum,* are purely ornamental plants.

Each nine-panel set is composed of three rows of three panels. The twelve sets above the main part of the Hall each have the lower and middle rows covered by a single design with the name of the species represented on the beam below. The remaining six sets above the stairs and landing at the south end of the Hall have a different plant depicted in each panel of the lower and middle rows, also labelled with the Latin name of the species. Every panel in the top row throughout the Hall has a separate illustration of a rather stylized plant. These are the "designs ... of an archaic character" mentioned in *The British Architect* and are not named on the panels. True to the original concept, they are the most brightly painted of the panels. Thirty-six similar panels arranged in sets of six with an upper row of three panels and a lower row of three roof the smaller North Hall. Like those above the Central Hall, the uppermost rows are brightest, but here they contain the heraldic plants of England, Ireland and Scotland; a rose, a shamrock and a thistle respectively. The panels in the lower rows show medicinal plants found wild in the British Isles.

Although the ceiling must have been a spectacular sight for the first visitors to the South Kensington building, the ravages of time eventually caught up with it, and by 1924 the ceiling was in a sorry state. The colours were faded, the panels dirty and in places cracked and damaged by leaks through the roof. A renovation programme that included cleaning the terracotta in the Hall repaired the damage, but some fifty years on roof failure again threatened the paintings. A second bout of repair work began in 1975, fittingly Architectural Heritage Year. For more than a year the ceiling was hidden from view above a soaring and intricate framework of scaffolding, but on 5th October 1976 the glorious sight that greeted those first visitors in 1881 was again available to the eyes of the public.

......
The vast framework of scaffolding needed to clean and repair the terracotta and ceiling in 1924.

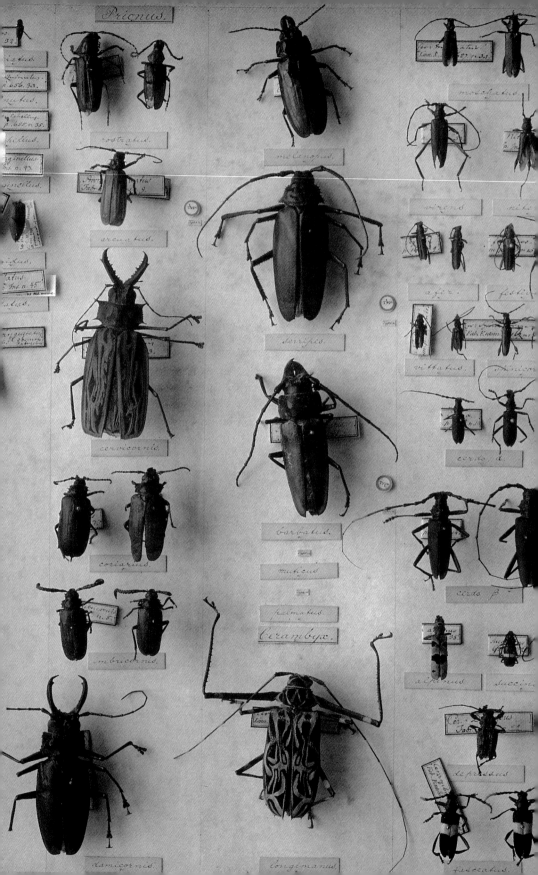

Prionus.

rostratus.

melanopus.

moschatus.

arcuatus.

serripes.

cervicornis.

vittatus.

coriarius.

barbatus.

muticus.

haimatus.

Cerambyx.

imbricornis.

alpinus.

succini.

depressus.

damicornis.

longimanus.

fasciatus.

CHAPTER : 5

THE COLLECTIONS:
BUILDING THE TREASUREHOUSE

Museums are all about objects. Any museum worthy of the name will have as its first priority the acquisition, care and conservation of a particular type of object, whether they be oil paintings, furniture, archaeological remains or natural history specimens. The Natural History Museum is no exception. As we have seen, the British Museum was founded to house the Sloane Collection, and the Act of Parliament of 1753 states "That within the Cities of London or Westminster, ... one general Repository shall be erected or provided ... for the Reception not only of the said Museum or Collection of Sir Hans Sloane, but also of the Cottonian Library, and of the Additions which have been or shall be made thereunto ..., and likewise of the said Harleian Collection of Manuscripts, ... which several collections, Additions, and Library so received into the said general Repository shall remain and be preserved therein for public Use to all Posterity". The collection grew by a series of haphazard donations until heads of department such as the zoologist John Edward Gray set out to collect systematically to try to ensure a good coverage of specimens across the whole range of his subject. These collections were displayed to the public in the British Museum galleries, they were studied by visiting naturalists, and they were used by staff to produce catalogues of different animal, mineral and plant groups.

The Museum houses more than 70 million specimens, many of them of great historical value, such as these beetles collected by Sir Joseph Banks.

By the time the new building in South Kensington was complete, these collections were vast and varied, and an enormous amount of planning must have gone into moving all the specimens. The minerals came first, 50,000 of them, all carefully wrapped and boxed, to be laid out in the great Mineral Gallery, where they still remain. Plants came next, including the 338 volumes of the Sloane Herbarium, the 25,000 sheets holding the collection of Sir Joseph Banks, Thomas Horsfield's plants from Java, 170,000 specimens from the collection of Robert Shuttleworth, and much else. The fossils followed soon afterwards, and were logistically much more of a problem, including, as they did, the huge fossil reptiles from the Thomas Hawkins collection, the fragile bones of the Missouri mastodon, the very valuable *Archaeopteryx* slabs, and countless tiny fossil shells, teeth and bones. All this material was in place by the time the Museum opened in April 1881. The zoological collections had to wait until the summer of 1882 to start their move, which was accomplished in 394 trips by horse and cart spread over ninety-seven days. The range of material transported was extraordinary, from great whale bones and stuffed animals to tiny shells and countless microscope slides. Fifty-two thousand glass bottles holding fish and other animals preserved in spirit had to be moved with special care. This was material collected from all over the world by many

of the great naturalists of the 19th century, including Charles Darwin, Alfred R. Wallace and John Gould. Seen as a whole the new Natural History Museum in South Kensington was the home to the finest and most comprehensive natural history collection in the world, built up to demonstrate the beauty, range and variety of nature.

. . . . . .
How The Comic News *imagined the forthcoming move of the zoological specimens to South Kensington. The reality was somewhat different.*

In many ways the material that came over to South Kensington from the British Museum was like a vast private collection, albeit one gathered together by a whole array of clergymen, travellers, wealthy amateurs, dukes and baronets. Specimens were of a high 'museum quality', acquired for their beauty, completeness and rarity. They came from many parts of the world, but principally from the countries of the old British Empire, although the places where they had been found were often not recorded in any detail. On the whole the larger and more showy animals and plants were better represented than the smaller and more ordinary. It was a collection for the general public to admire in the galleries and for scientists to use to describe and name genera and species, those units of description for the natural world that had been understood since the days of Linnaeus, more than a hundred years earlier. Species were seen as static and clearly separated from each other, definable in terms of the shape, colour and size. Specimens in the Museum became the basis for many thousands of original descriptions of this sort, becoming

Specimens and display cases brought to the rear of the Museum entered the building via the basement. They could be moved to other floors using the large trap and hoist in the Central Hall (shown here in 1933). It is still in use today.

'type specimens' in the process, and conferring an added importance to the whole collection by their presence. A type specimen is the unique representative of its particular species and the specimen to which the scientific name is correlated. Once defined, a type specimen remains forever of key value, and will be required for study whenever that species comes under review.

Twentieth-century taxonomy – as the process of naming in natural history is called – was to become very different. The concept of species became less all-encompassing, so that a single Victorian species might be subdivided into ten or even a hundred more closely defined species, meaning that collecting needed to be much more systematic and detailed. The incredible wealth of species in groups like the insects also became recognized, as the tropical and submarine worlds began to be explored in detail. In mineralogy, physical and chemical techniques led to the discovery of many new forms, quite invisible in the old hand specimens. At the same time the variety of form and colour within each species began to be appreciated, so that a single specimen could no longer adequately define it, and many hundred specimens might be needed to describe the full range of variation hidden within a single name. Variety across the geographical range of a species meant

TYPE

that accurate locality and ecological information became crucial. The final problem was that the huge increase in taxonomic work going on all over the world meant that the possibility of error increased dramatically. The same species might be given different names by different scientists, specific names might be misspelt in print, leading to endless confusion, and different species might be confused and lumped together. The need for care and caution became ever greater. On top of this came the realization that even The Natural History Museum could never be truly comprehensive, and that it would be better to concentrate efforts on groups of medical, agricultural or other importance, such as aphids, soil mites and parasitic worms, rather than to collect indiscriminately. These changes in science led to changes in the way the Museum went about building up its collections. Gifts and purchases from individuals were still important,

. . . .

*A type specimen
is the material
used to make
the first scientific
description
of a species.
This one is of
a Himalayan
species of Jasmin.*

but they were overshadowed by the results of specially mounted scientific expeditions that set out with carefully defined research objectives and were followed up by lavish publications. The finds may not always have been visually spectacular, but they have given The Natural History Museum's collection the extraordinary depth and richness that makes it unique today.

A detailed description of the thousands of acquisitions made by the Museum during its time in South Kensington is outside the scope of a short history. However, by picking just a few examples it is possible to indicate the extraordinary range of material that has come in over the years, as well as the different types of people and organizations that have been the Museum's benefactors.

The Osteological Gallery in 1893.
As well as complete skeletons, such as
the hippopotamus in the foreground,
the gallery contained numerous sets
of horns displayed on the tops of the
wall-cases.

Among the expeditions that made a major impact on the Museum's collections during this period are the round the world voyage of the *Challenger* (1872–1874), the British Ornithologists Union Expedition to Papua New Guinea (1909–1911), Captain Scott's British Antarctic Expedition in the *Terra Nova* (1910), the Museum's own expedition to the dinosaur-bearing deposits of Tanganyika (1924–1931), the Great Barrier Reef Expedition (1928–1929), the John Murray Expedition to the Indian Ocean (1933–1934), and the Royal Society Southern Pacific Expedition to the Solomon Islands (1964–1966).

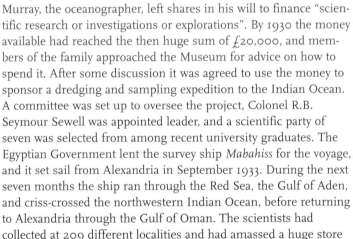

. . . .

The Challenger *scientists collected tens of thousands of speciemens including these rat-tails from the deep Pacific.*

. . . .

The Mabahiss, *generously loaned to the John Murray Expedition by the Egyptian Government.*

The John Murray Expedition can be the example that stands for the others. Sir John Murray, the oceanographer, left shares in his will to finance "scientific research or investigations or explorations". By 1930 the money available had reached the then huge sum of £20,000, and members of the family approached the Museum for advice on how to spend it. After some discussion it was agreed to use the money to sponsor a dredging and sampling expedition to the Indian Ocean. A committee was set up to oversee the project, Colonel R.B. Seymour Sewell was appointed leader, and a scientific party of seven was selected from among recent university graduates. The Egyptian Government lent the survey ship *Mabahiss* for the voyage, and it set sail from Alexandria in September 1933. During the next seven months the ship ran through the Red Sea, the Gulf of Aden, and criss-crossed the northwestern Indian Ocean, before returning to Alexandria through the Gulf of Oman. The scientists had collected at 209 different localities and had amassed a huge store of data and specimens. Crucial to the Museum had been the agreement of the Committee that The Natural History Museum would oversee publication of the scientific results of the expedition, and receive the pick of the collection. William Calman, Keeper of Zoology, acted as General Editor, and

through 1934 the huge collection arrived at the Museum. Increasing specialization in natural history meant that a large number of scientists would be involved in identifying the specimens and writing up the results for publication. Calman, with his wide range of contacts, was ideally placed to divide up the great mass of material and send portions out to specialists all over the world. These specialists were busy people, with desks already covered with work waiting to be done, but nonetheless, by 1939, when war broke out, a good start had already been made, with twenty-five reports already published, and the collections they related to safely lodged back in the Museum. The War slowed down progress dramatically, and it was not until 1946 that Hampton Parker, who took over as General Editor, was able to pick up the threads and try to discover what was going on. He was dismayed to discover that some of his workers had retired, some moved on to other fields of interest, while others simply went quiet and did not answer his ever patient letters. "Getting blood out of a stone" is a phrase that begins to appear in the correspondence files. Some collections were returned to the Museum to be reassigned to new authors, while the screws were tightened on those who continued to promise results. More members of the Museum's own staff were drafted in to help. The whole process dragged on beyond even Parker's retirement, but eventually, in 1967, the final part of the *Scientific Reports of the John Murray Expedition to the Indian Ocean* was published, doubtless to sighs of relief all round. The tens of thousands of specimens, mostly bottled animal specimens in spirits, could now be preserved as a priceless collection of reference data.

. . . . . .
Scientists and crew of the Mabahiss *recovering samples obtained by dredging and trawling.*

Of the many private benefactors who have enriched the Museum, Walter, 2nd Baron Rothschild, stands head and shoulders above the rest, both in the size and importance of his bequest. Born into the great banking family, Walter showed an early love of natural history, but absolutely no aptitude for business. His father built him a museum at the corner of Tring Park, the family home, and, after just a few years struggling with the mysteries of banking, he was allowed to pursue his passion undisturbed. Being a wealthy man, he was able to sponsor collectors in many parts of the world, as well as mounting his own expeditions to North Africa and elsewhere. His chief areas of expertise were the insects, of which he built up a vast collection of butterflies and moths; birds, which he was forced to sell to America in 1931 to pay off his mounting debts; and large animals, such as the gorilla and the giant tortoise. His museum, managed by professional curators, was open to the public from 1891, although Rothschild himself became increasingly shy and reclusive. He was well known at

. . . .
Lord Rothschild, founder of the Zoological Museum at Tring, riding on the back of a giant tortoise.

*The Zoological
Museum, Tring,
in 1899.*

· · · · · ·
*The bird
collections at
Tring hold about
1 million bird
skins representing
well over 95%
of known species,
as well as some
17,000 specimens
preserved in
spirit, over
14,000 skeletons,
about 1 million
eggs and
2000 nests.*

The Natural History Museum as both a collector and a scientist, and was elected a Trustee in 1899. It must have been sometime in the 1920s that he decided to leave his entire museum, every case, specimen and label, to The Natural History Museum, and on his death in 1937 this, the most magnificent single gift in the Museum's history, was received. It comprised buildings and land at Tring; a large display collection of stuffed mammals, birds, reptiles and fish, displayed in galleries that are still open to the public today; research collections that included an estimated 2.5 million butterflies and moths and 2000 bird skins; and a magnificent library of manuscripts and printed books. From this date Tring became a valued out-station of the Museum in South Kensington, which was used for evacuated storage during the War, and which now houses the Sub-Department of Ornithology.

In complete contrast to the huge and varied Rothschild Collection is the Ashcroft Collection of Swiss minerals. Frederick Noel Ashcroft took up mineral collecting while a student at Oxford, and collected among the volcanic rocks of Northern Ireland for a number of seasons before the First World War. He went on holiday to Switzerland with his family in 1921 and became interested in the minerals of that country, realizing that, although all the main mineral types were well known in collections, the exact places where they were found were only rarely recorded. Encouraged by L.J. Spencer, a mineralogist at the Museum, Ashcroft decided to build up a collection where every specimen would be of the highest quality and precisely localized. He concentrated on a relatively small area of southern Switzerland and, as the range of species occurring was fairly limited, he could aim to be complete and comprehensive. Each year he spent the summer in Switzerland, getting to know all the local collectors and buying their very best specimens. He made it a rule to visit and photograph the place where each specimen had been found, making detailed notes on the circumstances of the find in what developed into a great catalogue, almost as valuable as the specimens themselves. He did not keep any of his specimens for very long, but every few years made gifts of them to the Museum, where they soon built up into a collection that the Swiss themselves came to England to see. By the time he died in 1949 at the age of seventy, Ashcroft had ensured that the finest and best-documented collection of the minerals of southern Switzerland in existence was safely housed in The Natural History Museum, where it will stay to delight connoisseurs of fine minerals forever.

. . . . . .
Ashcroft meticulously recorded details relating to his collections in his notebooks.

Edward Meyrick, too, could hardly have been more different from Lord Rothschild. The son of a English clergyman, he was a schoolmaster for all his working life, firstly in Sydney, Australia, then in Christchurch, New Zealand, before he returned to England in 1886 to teach Latin and Greek for twenty-eight years at Marlborough College, his own old school. It is extraordinary that,

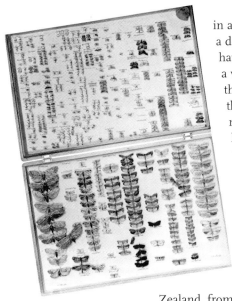

in addition to building a successful career in a demanding field, Meyrick should also have found the time and energy to become a world expert on the Microlepidoptera, those small and rather dull-looking moths that are scarcely noticed but teem in great numbers around the world. He published his first paper on the group in 1875, when he was only twenty-one, and his last in 1938, shortly before he died at the age of eighty-four. In all he published over 400 books and papers, and even published his own journal, which he called *Exotic Microlepidoptera,* and which consisted entirely of papers written by himself. He described these moths from Australia and New Zealand, from the South Pacific, Algeria, South Africa, India, Burma and Malaya, and by the end of his life there was hardly any part of the world that had not attracted his attention. During all this time he also collected the moths he described, many by his own hands, but with large numbers sent to him by correspondents and fellow enthusiasts. It was said that he hardly ever needed to visit The Natural History Museum, having all the material required for his researches in his own study. He described and named around 20,000 Lepidoptera during his sixty years of work, and many of the type specimens were to be found in his own, meticulously curated collection. He was not well known outside the very narrow circle of microlepidopterists, living quietly in Marlborough during his long retirement and working, as he always had done, until an hour after midnight. After his death his widow offered his collection to the Museum, where it was received with enthusiasm, transforming the holdings of this group into a world-class resource. The collection comprised almost 100,000 specimens, and is still being actively worked on today.

Not all important acquisitions have been in the form of whole collections of course. Like all the science departments, Palaeontology offers an enquiry and information service, and all through the day the door is opened to admit school pupils, family groups, students and other collectors eager to show off their finds. But just occasionally, in among the flints, pieces of ammonite, broken sea urchins and belemnite guards, there is a real treasure.

Trevor Batchelor arrived out of the blue on 1st February 1983 carrying a large, heavy, claw-like object, nearly 30 cm (1 foot) long. It was clearly part of a fossil vertebrate, and, as it had been found in Cretaceous rocks, was likely to be a reptile, and most probably part of a dinosaur. It had been found a month or so earlier by Mr Batchelor's father-in-law, Bill Walker, an enthusiastic amateur collector, who had been searching the Ockley Brick Company's claypit in Surrey. He saw a large lump of rock with an exposed piece of bone, broke it up with his hammer, carefully collected all the fragments and, taking them home, was able to cement them together to form the huge claw, that was now being examined with great excitement by the Museum's dinosaur experts, Alan Charig and Angela Milner. The following week the two of them visited the claypit with Bill and his daughter as their guides. Digging through the wet clay close to where the claw had been found, further large bones were revealed. This was clearly a major find. The actual excavation, by kind permission of the Company, took place once the clay had dried out at the end of May, and involved eight palaeontologists from the Museum, together with various

· · · · · · ·
Bill Walker holding the claw of Baryonix walkeri. *Behind him is the reconstructed skeleton.*

enthusiastic volunteers. The bones were preserved in about fifty hard siltstone nodules, weighing a total of 2 tonnes, each of which had to be wrapped and protected before being carefully transported to the Museum's Conservation Laboratory for the long process of preparing the skeleton. As it emerged the skeleton surpassed everyone's wildest dreams. It was truly the most important dinosaur discovery in Europe of the 20th century, representing an entirely unknown type of flesh-eating theropod, the only one known from rocks of Early Cretaceous age anywhere in the world. The find was christened "Claws", and received huge press coverage. Later a scientific paper formally named the beast *Baryonix*

walkeri (heavy claw of Walker). And it all sprung from the extraordinary piece of good fortune that Bill Walker just happened to be at the right place at the right time, otherwise the whole skeleton would have been crushed and incorporated into bricks!

From time to time The Natural History Museum has received entire museums, transferred from organizations that can no longer look after them, or no longer see them as central to their current concerns.

. . . .

Preparation of the Baryonix *skeleton in the Palaeontology Laboratory at the Museum.*

. . . .

The main hall and galleries of the Geological Museum as they appeared in 1963.

The Royal Society's cabinet of curiosities was acquired in the 18th century, and the Zoological Society and the East India Company's museums in the 19th. One of the greatest acquisitions of this type came right at the end of the 20th century, and was linked to the merger with the Geological Museum that took place in 1985. The Geological Museum has a long and distinguished history all of its own, having been founded in 1832 as the Museum of Economic Geology under the Office of Woods and Forests, to house the collections of the newly founded Ordnance Geological Survey, a body responsible for constructing geological maps of the country. The Survey moved out of London to new headquarters near Nottingham in 1980, leaving the Geological Museum out on a limb, and in 1985 it was merged with its next-door neighbour, The Natural History Museum, where it now forms the Earth Galleries. All the collections needed for the Survey's own research were removed to Keyworth, its new headquarters. However, it was agreed that minerals, building stones and certain historic rock collections should be transferred to The Natural History Museum along with the Geological Museum itself. The three collections ended up in the Mineralogy Department, where they significantly

enriched its holdings. The minerals, 30,000 in all, included a magnificent suite of rough and cut gemstones, wonderful British material from the collection of Henry Ludlam, and a significant number of meteorites. The collection of building stones, for long a speciality of the Geological Museum, owed its formation to the search for stone for the rebuilding of the Houses of Parliament in the 1830s, and has been consulted by architects ever since, while the historic rock collections derived from the Geological Society's Museum, which was acquired in 1911. The specimens are mostly small and unprepossessing, but were collected by the greatest names in the early days of British geology, such as Adam Sedgwick, Roderick Murchison, Charles Lyell and William Buckland, and often illustrated the papers that they published.

. . . .
Excavations
at Piltdown.

. . . .
A reconstruc-
tion of the
Piltdown
skull. The
darker pieces
represent the
original frag-
ments which
consisted of
a human
cranium and
the jaw of a
modern ape.

The Natural History Museum has acquired a few things that it has subsequently regretted, of course, as is inevitable in such a huge operation. The Piltdown skull, for example, presented by Charles Dawson in 1912, and described as the most important fossil ever discovered, caused no end of mischief before it was finally proved to be a fake in 1953. A more serious problem is posed by the collections of Richard Meinertzhagen, acquired in 1954. Meinertzhagen joined the army in 1899, served as an Intelligence Officer with the Egyptian Expeditionary Force, attended the Paris Peace Conference in 1919 and held military posts with the Foreign Office until 1925 when he retired to devote himself to ornithology. He was described by an earlier historian of the Museum as colourful, adventurous, cunning and unscrupulous. He was associated with the Museum throughout his life, being a regular visitor to the "Bird Room". He was often fiercely critical of the Museum, and was regarded with some suspicion by the staff, being suspected of "borrowing" specimens without authority on several occasions. However, early problems were smoothed over, and he was made

an Honorary Associate, and presented his library together with his huge collection of bird skins, bird lice and plants in 1954, many of which were displayed in a special gallery named in his honour. Recent research has raised serious doubts about the integrity of the collection of bird skins. Some specimens have falsified localities, others had been stolen from the Museum's own collection and renamed and relabelled, again with a new locality. These frauds have only been proved for a small number of the 25,000 specimens, but they are enough to cast a doubt on everything bearing the name Meinertzhagen Collection.

. . . .
The vast majority of the Museum's specimens are not on public display, but form the basis of research projects by scientists.

    The vast collections held in The Natural History Museum, now totalling more than 70 million specimens, are used for many different purposes. A large number are still displayed in the Museum galleries or used in lectures and demonstrations as part of the Museum's important role in public education and recreation. A much larger number form the basis of research projects being carried out by the Museum's own staff and by the various voluntary and associate workers who contribute so much to the work of the Museum. In addition, a large number of visitors come from all over the world to work on the collections, some for just a few days and others for a year or more. Some are students working towards a postgraduate degree, others are senior figures

Bernard
Woodward
(seated right)
and his staff in
the General
Library, 1909.

from museums and universities. There is also an enormous loans service whereby specimens are dispatched by post or by courier, once again to organizations all over the world. But the value of the collections cannot be judged in terms of those specimens that are studied in any one year, for the collections are a great and irreplaceable data store that will serve the needs of future scientists for generations, and will provide research data for projects as yet undreamed of.

One very important collection that has not yet been mentioned is the Library. The Natural History Museum Library, with its huge store of printed books, periodicals, manuscripts, drawings and electronic resources, exists to support and enable the curatorial, research and educational work of the Museum. The Museum arrived in South Kensington without any library worthy of the name. The Trustees of the British Museum had decided that the natural history books in the Department of Printed Books would stay in Bloomsbury, and that only the small departmental libraries, amounting to just a few thousand items, would be allowed to go. This faced the new museum with a real problem, and the authorities were lucky to persuade Parliament to make a series of annual grants to build up a General Library and the four, later five, specialist departmental libraries. Bernard Woodward was transferred from Bloomsbury to take charge of the growing collection, and by the time he retired in 1920 the Library had an international reputation. Natural history of the type practised within the Museum differs from the other sciences in that the older literature holds its value over the years. A paper in which a new species is named and described is important, whether it was published in 1800, 1900 or last year. For this reason, the Library's valuable collection of rare books, such as the wonderful monograph on parrots illustrated by Edward Lear, the great folios of John Gould, and, supremely, Audubon's *Birds of America*, are just as much a part of the working collection as the modern reference books and journals. The Library is rich in manuscripts and drawings that, once again, supplement the scientific work of the Museum.

. . . .
The blue and yellow maccaw, painted by Edward Lear, 1832.

The correspondence of Lord Rothschild for example, held in the General Library, documents his activities as a collector, and can provide information about the localities and origin of important specimens in his collection. The wonderful collection of watercolour drawings, which comes as such a surprise to many of the Museum's visitors, includes depictions of exotic animals drawn at a time when no specimens were known in Europe, or of specimens where the originals are now lost. While stressing scientific significance, no one would deny the sheer beauty of the Australian animal paintings of Ferdinand Bauer, the more homely charm of the work of William MacGillivray, or the sheer inventiveness of Olivia Tonge. These are things to delight as well as to instruct.

Conservation of these many and varied collections imposes a heavy burden on the Museum. Many specimens are fragile and will not stand handling, while others are unstable and will decay under "normal" room conditions. Still others are vulnerable to attack by mould, insects and other pests. Constant vigilance by teams of curators is needed to ensure that the collections remain in good condition for the future.

Some techniques for preparing or restoring fragile specimens such as herbarium specimens have changed little over the years. The equipment in the plant mounting room in 1934 is still in daily use.

The Spirit Building

In the northwest corner of the South Kensington site stood a four-storey building of distinctly utilitarian appearance. This unprepossessing edifice was the New Spirit Building and concealed one of the most impressive parts of the Museum's collections. Here were specimens of mammals, reptiles, fish, mites, spiders, sponges and a great many others, preserved mainly in spirit (70–80% industrial methylated spirit).

The sixteen storerooms contained 25 km (15.5 miles) of shelving, and 400,000 glass jars ranging in height from a few centimetres to over a metre and holding in all some 350,000 litres (77,000 gallons) of spirit. The figure for the number of individual specimens, estimated at 22 million, was even more impressive.

The original Spirit Building stood on the northeast side of the South Kensington site. Among all the detailed plans for the original Waterhouse building a surprising oversight was the omission of any provision for the spirit collections, which even then occupied three large rooms in the basement at Bloomsbury and which had already been identified as a major fire hazard. The belated solution jointly worked out by the Keeper of Zoology, Albert C. Günther, and the architect, Waterhouse, was to erect an additional, fire-proof building detached from the main Museum. The extra cost of over £20,000 predictably alarmed the Treasury but not sufficiently to prevent the plan going ahead, and the new building provided a home for these collections for the next half century.

The New Spirit Building on the north-west corner of the museum, photographed in 1930.

The New Spirit Building was constructed piecemeal over a period of seventeen years, beginning in 1921 when work on the first half was instigated. In 1924 all of the Zoology spirit collections with the exception of fishes were transferred there. The new building, more precisely half a building, brought to an end a "condition of paralysing congestion which had become

acute even as long ago as 1914". This happy situation was short-lived, and on 5th December 1930 the Archbishop of Canterbury formally opened a much-needed extension. The funding had been provided by the Empire Marketing Board, but on the understanding that the extension was to be occupied by the grossly overcrowded insect collections until permanent accommodation could be provided for them. In 1933 a second extension was planned, together with a completely new building referred to as the New Western Block. These were both completed in 1935 and a year later the New Western Block became home to the bird and insect collections, including those temporarily housed in the Spirit Building. As a last fillip, mezzanine floors were installed in the Spirit Building, the whole of which was now available for the spirit collections. Finally, in 1938, the fish specimens languishing in the old Spirit Building were moved to rejoin the remainder of the spirit collections in the new building.

The New Spirit Building was the last in its line and demolition of it began in 2001. By then the ever-expanding spirit collections had been transferred yet again, this time to the Darwin Centre building where purpose-designed accommodation provides better storage and access.

. . . .
Part of the collection of fishes in the New Spirit Building.

CHAPTER : 6

EXHIBITONS AND EDUCATION:
REACHING THE AUDIENCE

The Natural History Museum collections have always been on show to the public. Sloane's original vision was of a collection that was for the benefit of the public as well as the expert naturalist, and so it has always been. Visitors to Montagu House saw the whole Sloane Collection laid out in glass-fronted cases or on open tables, and they loved it. Even after the move to the new building in the 1830s, it was still assumed that the whole collection should be displayed if possible, and only the insects were hidden away "behind the scenes". As the collections grew the displays got more and more crowded until it was hardly possible to see the wood for the trees. There was no scope for arrangement or attractive display, as the maximum number of objects had to be squeezed into the smallest possible space. Labels were rudimentary, and visitors had to rely on the densely printed *Synopsis*, which was on sale for one shilling, for any real information. In spite of these shortcomings, the natural history displays were enormously popular, and attracted large crowds on all public holidays. The large stuffed mammals were by far the most popular exhibits, not surprisingly in the days before natural history films and mass tourism.

Planning for the new museum in South Kensington inevitably led to discussion of the purpose of the public galleries and the way to make them most effective. Richard Owen, who was head of the Natural History Departments at the Museum, believed that the galleries should accurately reflect the natural world itself, and that specimens of every known animal, mineral and vegetable should be freely available for the public to see. He scorned the idea that one antelope might be more important than another, believing that all antelopes must be on display, both male and female, young and old. He believed strongly in the moral benefit of natural history displays, in that careful study of the works of the Creator would inevitably lead to a better understanding of God himself. With this in mind, Owen designed a museum that was very large,

The Museum's first Guide Lecturer, John Leonard, with a party of visitors in one of the galleries.

and consisted almost entirely of public galleries, with just a few offices for staff. He did, however, advocate an introductory area for those without the time or the background knowledge to cope with the main galleries. Opposing Owen were most other naturalists, who believed that the public only needed to see carefully selected examples from the natural world, and that most of the collections should be reserved for the use of students and other specialists. They believed that it was the job of the professional curator to make the selection and thus to guide and inform the visiting public. A museum designed with this philosophy in mind would be smaller overall than Owen's model, and have smaller public areas but extensive storage and study space.

When the new Museum opened in South Kensington in 1881 it could be seen that Owen had largely carried the day. The Museum as built was large, with an imposing 600 foot (183 m) frontage, and, with the exception of storage areas in the basement, was entirely composed of public galleries. These galleries were of two types, a distinction that survived right until the 1970s. On the one hand were large galleries devoted to a single class of object, such as the minerals, fossils, mammals or birds. These were the jealously guarded responsibility of the keeper of the relevant science department, who would generally allow no inter-ference, particularly from Richard Owen or his successors, and admit of no collaboration or consultation. On the other hand were the entrance areas comprising the Central and North Halls, which were introductory in character and were the responsibility of the Director – the only exhibition area that he could truly "direct".

. . . .

One of the ground floor public galleries in 1931. This contains exhibits of birds, while smaller ones leading off it display corals, reptiles, insects and other groups.

Owen's original idea for this central area was that it should contain a display of typical specimens and would function as an introduction, or index, to the Museum as a whole – hence its later name, the Index Museum. It was to be an area for visitors without the time or the necessary knowledge to appreciate the more demanding departmental galleries. It could also be an area where senior staff would give lectures and demonstrations to the public, and might even be opened in the evenings for the benefit of working men and others who were unable to visit during the week. If the Museum were an epitome of the natural world, then the Index Museum was to be an epitome of the Museum.

The reality was rather different. The problem with the Index Museum was that neither Owen nor his successors were capable, or really interested, in producing simple, straightforward exhibits requiring little previous knowledge. They were more concerned with showing off the wonders of science. The bay devoted to birds, which was completed by Owen in 1882, survives in part to the present day. It contained material on the structure and comparative anatomy of the wing, the physiology of sight and hearing, the structure of the feather and other topics, all fascinating and important, but hopelessly complex, and surely above the heads of the working men and their families of the day. The height of absurdity was reached in 1910 when it was decided that the Index Museum needed an introductory case for those who might find the main displays within it too complex! With the Index Museum displays confined to the side bays of the Central Hall, there was still the huge central space to be filled. This has always demanded the largest possible exhibit, initially the skeleton of a sperm whale from Caithness, Scotland, later elephants and other pachyderms, and, most recently, the great *Diplodocus carnegeii* cast. But alongside this great single object came a whole miscellany of temporary displays on odd biological topics that did not quite fit elsewhere in the Museum.

· · · · · ·
The large 'stuffed beasts' have always been major attractions in the Museum. Even moving them in or out of the building, as this elephant in need of restuffing in 1927 shows, can draw quite a crowd.

The Index Museum, shown here in 1895, was only the side bays of the Central Hall. The open area in the middle was reserved for very large specimens and smaller, temporary exhibits.

Among the earliest were displays on camouflage, on mimicry, on albinism and adaptation to the snow, and on domestic and fancy pigeons, while during the First World War came popular displays on the army biscuit and on the flea. These were topics that did not fit neatly into the departmental galleries, or that the Director wished to highlight for some reason of his own.

The departmental galleries led off the Central Hall and its balconies: Geology, Mineralogy and Botany to the east, and Zoology to the west. They were large, but certainly not comprehensive in Owen's sense of the word. They presented a generous selection from the natural world, but never attempted to display examples of every species or even of every genus. Right from the beginning departments made a division between specimens for display and those for storage and study, with the proportion of those for display becoming steadily smaller as the research collections grew and grew. Galleries were in all cases laid out taxonomically, so that the classification and subdivision of the group in question was clear to see. Thus, for example, the Fish Gallery was divided first between the bony and the cartilaginous fishes, and then subdivided to show examples of all the different families of these groups. There must have been close to a thousand specimens of fish on display. In spite of this rigorously scientific approach, keepers went to considerable trouble to make the galleries interesting and accessible to the public. Labels were

more informative than they had been in the old British Museum, and were backed up by maps and other diagrams. Furthermore, most of the galleries were provided with an inexpensive guidebook, which gave background information about the group in question. In many ways the departmental galleries were more accessible than the supposedly introductory Index Museum.

Four of the Museum's most popular exhibits deserve detailed description: the skeletons of the horse and man, the sequoia slice, the *Diplodocus* cast and the blue whale model.

Sir William Henry Flower, the first Director of the Museum.

William Henry Flower was appointed to succeed Richard Owen in 1884 and was given the new title of Director. He was an anatomist who had seen service in the Crimean War, worked at the Middlesex Hospital, and served for some years as Conservator at the Royal College of Surgeons in Lincoln's Inn Fields in London. Here he had paid a great deal of attention to making the displays not only scientifically accurate, but attractive and easy to understand. He took great trouble over colour, typography, the wording of labels and the layout of specimens within a showcase. He ensured that the case was never crowded, so that each object could be clearly seen and could make its own particular point. Flower was also convinced of the reality of evolution by natural selection, and was a friend and follower of Charles Darwin. When he arrived at the Museum he must have felt that there was much to do! As we have seen, the only areas that he could take effective charge of were the Central and North Halls, and he set to work producing detailed displays on the adaptation of the teeth of mammals to their diet. However, it was in the North Hall that he set up his most telling and enduring exhibit. This was a tableau of a man leading a horse, with a dog in attendance, each figure being a skeleton partly clothed in flesh and skin. With the fewest possible words the display perfectly makes the point of the adaptation of the basic mammalian skeleton to different means of locomotion. It has moved several times during the last 110 years, and is currently displayed in the Mammal Gallery.

It was in 1892 that a unique opportunity arose, the chance to purchase from the Kings River Lumber Company a complete slice of a giant sequoia for display in the Museum. The tree selected grew in California. After felling, a section of the trunk 16 feet (5 m) in diameter, four and a half feet (1.4 m) thick and weighing 36 tons was shipped from San Francisco to Liverpool on the British boat *Candida*. The cost of the specimen was a mere $700. On arrival in London the section was split into several slices for presentation to other institutions, the best slice of course being kept in London. It was duly set up in the North Hall, where its sheer size ensured that it commanded immediate attention. A few years later someone was given the task of counting the 1335 or so rings in the wood and marking on a series of the most famous dates in

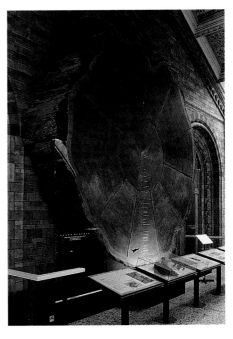

British history, so the visitor could see at a glance that in 1066 the tree was already over 7 feet (2.1 m) in diameter. Once again, with the minimum of words and explanation, it became a truly awe-inspiring exhibit. The sequoia slice now stands high above Central Hall on the Botany Landing.

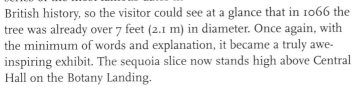

Now on the Botany Landing of the Central Hall, the sequoia is one of the landmark exhibits, used by visitors and staff alike to orient them-selves within the Museum.

The Museum has often benefited from its long association with the Royal Family, but perhaps never more than in 1903. King Edward VII had been an enthusiastic Trustee when he was Prince of Wales, and kept the Museum very much in mind once he became King. He visited the United States in 1903 and was a guest of the industrialist millionaire Andrew Carnegie. Carnegie showed the King illustrations of the great sauropod dinosaur *Diplodocus*, which had recently been named after him, and of which there was a complete cast mounted in the Carnegie Museum in Pittsburgh. King Edward immediately suggested that such a cast would make a very welcome addition to The Natural History Museum in London and Carnegie, with characteristic generosity, agreed to

have one prepared at his own expense. It was shipped to London in thirty-six large packing cases and was mounted in the Reptile Gallery under the supervision of W. J. Holland of the museum in Pittsburgh. With a length of 80 feet (24.4 m) and a height to the shoulders of 14 feet (4.3 m), *Diplodocus* single-handedly changed the popular view of the Museum from the "stuffed animal museum" to "the dinosaur museum". Once again, the great cast has been displayed in several different locations, and, as our understanding of these great creatures increased, has also had to be reposed. *Diplodocus* was originally thought to drag its tail along the ground, rather like a bridal train. We now know that the tail was carried parallel to but well clear of the ground. In 1993 the skeleton was remounted with new, lighter but stronger casts of the tail bones and hind legs. These had to be made using the original cast as a pattern and for three months *Diplodocus* suffered the indignity of wearing a paper tail until the work could be completed. It now stands, with tail aloft, as a fitting centrepiece to the great Central Hall.

A splendid new Whale Hall was built on the northern edge of the Museum site between 1930 and 1934, replacing the temporary shed that had been put up in the 1880s. This new building was strong enough to have the huge blue whale skeleton that had been in store since 1891 hanging from the roof. At 82 feet (25 m) long, this rivalled *Diplodocus* in size, reminding the public that there are still giants alive in the world's seas. Some representation of this great animal in life was clearly needed to complete the display.

A cast from a real animal was rejected as too expensive, and it was decided to build a model instead. Francis Fraser was the scientific supervisor, with Percy Stammwitz being in charge of the actual construction. The Hall remained open to the public while work was in progress, through 1937 and 1938, so the public could watch the vast animal take shape. The method used was similar to the way a First World War aeroplane was built, with huge wooden formers being framed and fastened, and then covered with wire mesh, plastered and eventually painted. There were many arguments among the staff along the way, particularly over the final colour, but by December 1938 a time capsule was sealed into the animal's belly, and all was finished. At 93 feet (28.3 m), it remains the largest single object in the Museum.

· · · · · ·
Fittingly, the model of the blue whale dwarfs the other animals attending it in the Whale Hall.

An important appointment was made in 1912 when John Leonard became the Museum's first Guide Lecturer. It was clear from simple observation that many visitors wandered aimlessly around the galleries without really gaining any benefit from the exhibits. A campaign in the pages of *The Times*, led by Lord Sudeley, spurred the Trustees into action, and Leonard was duly appointed, leading two one-hour tours each weekday. He was a great success, and became, as far as the visitors were concerned, the most important member of the staff. He seems to have had the knack of giving just the right amount of information for his particular group of visitors, and giving it in such a way as to make natural history seem the most fascinating subject in the world.

Visitors to the Earth Galleries are met
by a group of six symbolic statues,
each with accompanying specimens,
which introduce the main subjects
explained in the galleries beyond.

Over the years the educational activities organized within the Museum have diversified enormously. There were daily public lectures through much of the 1930s and 1940s; special lectures, films, demonstrations and tours through the 1950s; a Children's Centre was set up in 1948 with a series of clubs providing Saturday morning activities for the young; there were visits by large numbers of school parties, and courses specially arranged for teachers. In 1979 educational activities were made the responsibility of the newly formed Visitor Resources Section, and the strategy emerged that, any one exhibition being designed with a particular target audience, it would be the job of the Section to help make it useful and enjoyable for those outside the target. Thus an exhibition designed for adults with a high previous interest in birds might be provided with a set of children's worksheets, while one aimed at young teenagers would need more detailed literature and perhaps a series of lectures to realize its full potential.

All of these exhibitions had followed a "look and learn" model, where the visitor was informed by the objects on display and any accompanying labels. A departure from this approach came in 1977, with the opening of the Hall of Human Biology – "an exhibition of ourselves". The Museum's own research had shown that, while visitors still delighted in the traditional exhibits on offer, younger visitors especially were hungry for something more. Human Biology focused on modern humans and was the first interactive exhibition, encouraging the visitors to explore and provide some of the information for themselves. Muscle actions were demonstrated by visitors using their own arms to operate a model mirroring the limb movements. Senses and even the process of abstract thought were among the facets of the human condition explored from conception and birth to old age.

The idea of drawing the visitor into the exhibition itself has proved popular. Few exhibits are more relished than the earthquake room, where one can vicariously experience the effects of one of the most powerful forces of nature – frightening in reality but thrilling in the safety of a gallery exhibit. Human Biology also introduced the idea of exhibits dealing with a complete theme or concept rather than a single group of organisms, allowing complex interrelationships and processes to be explained. The Ecology and Evolution exhibitions fit this description, as does the recent redevelopment of the Earth Galleries (1996–1998) which deals with the Earth sciences and their significance to people.

The First Museum Guidebook

The building of the new Museum at South Kensington necessitated production of a new guidebook to the natural history collections to supplant that in use at their old home in Bloomsbury. The guide, printed in 1883 when all but the Zoology collections had moved to their new home, was available to visitors at a cost of four old pence (just under 2p). What did the purchaser receive for this princely sum? By today's standards, quite a lot. Entitled *A Guide to the Exhibition Galleries in the British Museum (Natural History), Cromwell Road, South Kensington,* it was bound in a blue paper cover and dealt only with the Departments of Geology and Palæontology, Mineralogy and Botany, yet still ran to an incredible 170 pages!

The contents included a brief account of the genesis of the new Museum, together with a list of benefactors who had donated specimens. A ground plan of the building was so detailed it included the locations of the boilers and, perhaps to reassure visitors of their safety and well-being, of the smoke shafts "for drawing off the vitiated air from various galleries contiguous thereto". These introductory matters were followed by sections devoted to the different departments, an index, a list of the British Museum publications including those for the collections at Bloomsbury, and a list of photographs purchasable at the Principal Librarian's office (which included busts of emperors, philosophers and nude studies by Old Masters).

The section on the Department of Botany was very brief, a mere four pages, the majority of which was devoted to explaining the arrangement of the various herbaria,

Illustrations in the Museum's Guidebook of 1883: a musk ox (left) and the skeleton of the gigantic Irish deer, described as the "King of the Deer tribe" (right).

or that portion of the Department "set aside for the use of persons engaged in the scientific study of plants". The remainder describes material in the public galleries, but the arrangement was still in progress and "not sufficiently advanced to permit the preparation of a guide to the cases at the time when these pages must go to press".

This was certainly not the case for the other departments, whose sections contain a wealth of detail concerning the many objects on display. The text consisted of a brief introduction to the subject followed by more lengthy pieces on each of the natural orders of animals, minerals or rocks as appropriate. Thirty-one figures depicted items ranging from skulls to complete skeletons, a drawing of the *Archaeopteryx* fossil to reconstructions of extinct animals as they would have appeared in life. Plans of the galleries showing the locations of individual showcases were augmented by lists precisely detailing their contents. There was an index to the minerals in the collections and a complete cata-logue of meteorites giving where and when each fell to Earth (or was found if the fall was unknown) and the weight of the item in grams.

Throughout the guide, the emphasis was as much on instruction as explanation. Explanatory labels and other means were adopted to "bring all the objects exhibited within the comprehension of all visitors". These objects were used to make a series of scientific points, backed up by the brief but cogent summaries in the guide. The style is probably a little too stiff and formal for modern visitors and, in places, is unashamedly superior in tone. But the sheer volume of information and its scholarly presentation both demanded the interest of the visitor and rejoiced in it.

. . . .
The guidebook described some amazing fossils, such as the skull of a giant extinct kangaroo. A human skull was drawn alongside it for comparison and is one fifth the size.

*Huge numbers
of specimens
may be needed
to enable
scientists to
evaluate the
full range of
variation in
particular
organisms.*

were often based exclusively on material held in the Museum's
collections. Assessing the full range of variation within a species
requires the study of many specimens and the Museum had them
in vast numbers, too many in fact for the permanent staff to deal
with. This was to have several effects on the way in which Museum
scientists worked.

The catalogues and monographs not only inspired interest
outside the Museum but marked it as the institute of choice
among collectors when considering where to bequeath their (often
expensively assembled) collections, since here they would continue
to receive expert attention. The opportunity for patrons to garner
a little reflected glory by contributing to such highly regarded
intellectual advances, no matter how indirectly, was hard to resist.
But Museum researchers were few in number and individuals
were often solely responsible for the collections of one or more
major groups of animals, plants, fossils or minerals. In 1882,
for example, the Department of Zoology employed only three entomologists (Entomology was not yet a separate department) to deal
with all of the insect collections, which were averaging over 25,000
additional specimens each year. The flow of new material entering
the Museum had became a deluge, which threatened to overwhelm

its research capacity. Allied to this was the increase in scientific literature that had to be consulted to properly carry out taxonomic work. It was no longer possible for any one individual to remain abreast of current scientific knowledge and undertake high quality research on such a large scale. Of necessity, specialization set in and researchers began to focus on smaller taxonomic groups and geographic areas. However, while research horizons contracted on one level, on another they were expanding. Experts now looked more deeply at smaller groups, which often contained many more species than in the time of their predecessors. The increase in numbers is due not only to the discovery of new species but also to the recognition that many of the original species in fact represent several separate taxa. There are a variety of reasons for this. Increased numbers of collections allow a more complete assess-ment of the range of variation to be made and a more meaningful classification to reflect this variation. This is one of the principal reasons for the continuation of collecting. Recognition of the importance of previously known but unregarded characters such as wing colour in live insects allied to characteristics made newly available by technological advances provided a wealth of additional information. While the principles of taxonomy remained the same, the data on which to draw was greater than ever.

. . . . . .

Items as uncomplicated as egg shells may show considerable variation.

A second change in research practices in the Museum began in 1902. A system of loaning specimens to assist the studies of specialists elsewhere was widely established in Europe but, strangely, was held to be counter to the interests of the Museum. The Director of the Museum, E. Ray Lankester, saw the advantages of joining this system and received permission to send out specimens to other experts but only from the enormous backlog of material awaiting identification. Types and other important specimens were also sent out for study, an act which was not, strictly speaking, legal but which the Department of Botany at least circumvented by the simple device of writing a question mark on each sheet, thereby suggesting doubts as to its identification. The loan procedure was eventually formalized by Government Bill and the Museum was able both to send and receive loans of material for study. The importance of this seem-ingly minor change lies in the fact that the collections of a single institute, no matter how large, are insufficient to illustrate the full range of biodiversity, and taxonomists need to study collections from institutes all over the world in order to gain as complete a picture of the organisms as possible.

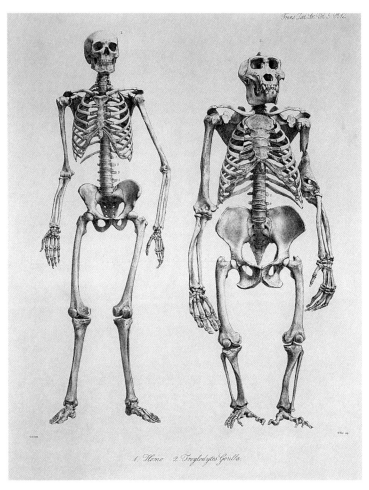

1. *Homo* 2. *Troglodytes Gorilla*

. . . .

Drawing by Richard Owen comparing human and gorilla skeletons. Darwins' theory of natural selection radically changed scientific views on evolution and descent.

The detail of descriptive taxonomy has changed little over the years and Sir Hans Sloane himself would be familiar with the form if not the content of modern Floras, Faunas and monographs. If the nuts and bolts of taxonomy remained essentially the same, this is certainly not true for other areas of research, particularly that relating to the study of evolution. Evolution is the history of life, and throughout the latter half of the 19th century and the first half of the 20th, fossils were seen as the most appropriate, indeed the only, means of tracing genealogical history. While one could see the results of evolution in present-day animals and plants, it was fossils that provided the proof of lines of descent. But all of this was to change, with the Museum playing a major part in the revolution.

After Darwin's successful introduction of his theory of natural selection, evolution became an increasingly important aspect of taxonomy. The process of evolution meant descent and implied relationships that could be expressed as family trees. The search was on for ancestors, missing links and other important genealogical evidence. But the means by which the closeness or otherwise of the relationships between species was assessed became more and more complex, involving the overall similarity of species, their distribution through the fossil record, their degree of difference and other intuitive measures. Using this methodology, a single lineage could be divided into a number of arbitrary divisions representing descendants. Overall or phenetic similarity is based simply on overall appearance and is not a rigorous criterion on which to build an evolutionary classification reflecting true descent from a common ancestor. Unrelated organisms may develop similar characteristics to deal with a common problem – for example the fins of fish and the flippers of whales. Such convergence can increase phenetic similarity to the point where different organisms are wrongly judged to be closely related genetically. Many scientists became dissatisfied with the subjective nature of this approach, including a number of those working at the Museum.

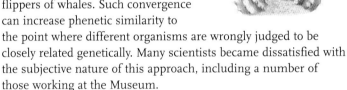

Overall (phenetic) similarity can mask true relationships. The cactus (left) and the spurge (right) have adapted to similar desert conditions and look alike, yet they are not related.

In 1966 the work of a German scientist, Willi Hennig, initially caught the attention of palaeontologists and later botanists and zoologists. Hennig attempted to provide a new approach that would enable a more scientific (i.e. testable) means of assessing relationships. By the 1970s this had given rise to a new school of evolutionary reconstruction and taxonomy called phylogenetic systematics – later to be known as cladistics – which departed methodologically from the traditional approach. Instead of searching for ancestors and their direct descendants, cladistics attempts to construct hierarchies of closest genealogical relatives or "sister groups" that reveal the relative order of branching in evolutionary history. From this history, a classification expressing the evolutionary relationships of the organisms is directly and unambiguously derived. Important as the relative merits of the two approaches were in terms of science, discussion of them would and perhaps should have remained confined to the esoteric realms of academic argument had not the Museum used the new, cladistic approach in a small exhibit on evolution involving man. In mimicry of Darwin's time, this emotive topic acted as a trigger for an unseemly row of unexpected proportions. Tensions between supporters and opponents of cladistic theory erupted. Between 1978 and 1981 the pages of the highly respected scientific journal *Nature* became a battlefield as the protagonists stated their cases and derided the ideas of the opposite camp. One of the leading science philosophers of the day, Karl Popper, was even dragged into the debate. The impassioned views expressed contained some remarkable accusations, including one that Museum scientists were using cladistics to pursue a hidden, Marxist, agenda and impose it upon unsuspecting and less articulate sections of the public! Eventually the furore died down and, as the insights provided by cladistic studies began to be more widely appreciated, it became the accepted approach to studying relationships. Outside scientific circles the controversy may have seemed little more than a minor spat between academics. Yet, in its way, this was the greatest upheaval in our understanding of evolution since Darwin.

. . . . . .
As part of its research the Museum monitors whale strandings in the UK. Scientists record as much information as possible before the carcass is removed.

During the 20th century research at the Museum was expanding into other disciplines. Although the Museum remained devoted primarily to the academic science of systematics, researchers were turning their attention to many aspects of the natural world. Changes in past climates, the structure and composition of minerals, the evolution of flight, courtship displays in birds, the role of sounds and mimicry in insects, and the structure and diversity of coral reefs are just a few of the subjects studied. Applied science in general came more strongly to the fore. For example, work on species conservation goes back as far as 1916 when the first in a series of studies on the protection of animals in areas affected by the First World War was carried out. Investigations into what is now referred to as sustainable usage,

including reports on whaling, sealing and the effects of the introduction of reindeer to the southern Atlantic island of South Georgia, were also carried out by Museum staff. One of the most important areas of applied research in terms of direct benefit to humans concerns pests and diseases.

What can a museum contribute to the understanding of diseases? The answer is a great deal, especially concerning the biology and control of vector-borne diseases, where the organism causing the disease is spread from victim to victim by a third party – the vector. A thorough knowledge of the vector is essential to combating the spread of the infection and the best examples occur among blood-sucking insects.

In the latter part of the 19th century the discoveries that both elephantiasis and malaria were mosquito-borne diseases marked the beginning of the science of medical entomology. They also signalled a peri-od of intense study of all potential vectors of similar diseases, studies that were to continue, using more and newer techniques, up to the present day.

At the beginning of the 1900s suspected disease-carrying insects could not even be identified (since few had been collected, let alone described), and the preparation of taxonomic monographs, especially on biting flies, was a priority for those studying human diseases in the field. The Museum was virtually the only place at which these essential monographs could be prepared, and the researchers in the entomology staff responded with remarkable speed, publishing between 1901 and 1911 works on mosquitoes, tsetse flies and other African blood-sucking insects. Later researchers continued the work by updating the rapidly advancing knowledge of mosquitoes in 1941 and producing monographs on African horseflies and blackflies in the 1950s.

The studies on blackflies illustrate how research can suddenly change direction. These small, biting flies are the vector for onchocerciasis or river blindness, a disease that affects some 17 million people worldwide. Up to the 1960s it was thought that physical characteristics alone were sufficient to ensure accurate identification of the different species of blackfly, yet baffling contradictions in the epidemiology of river blindness remained. It became clear that these could only be explained if so-called single species were in reality mixtures of several outwardly identical species each with its own environmental requirements,

. . . .
The mosquito
Aedes cantans,
painted by
Amadeo J.E.
Terzi c. 1937.
Mosquitoes are
among various
carriers of
disease which
have featured
in major
research
programmes at
the Museum.

biology and behaviour. The researchers had to look deeper. In the 1970s attention focused on the large chromosomes found in the flies' salivary glands. Differences in chromosomal structure revealed that the most important vector "species" in Africa comprises not one but over forty distinct races. For reasons that are still unclear, some of these races always transmit the disease while others do not. Current work in Central and South America is revealing a similar pattern of chromosomal races differing in both their behaviour and ability to transmit river blindness.

. . . .

The flea was one of the minor horrors of war featured by A.E. Shipley in his book of that name. The Museum's superb collection of fleas is used by experts around the world for research

The Museum's researchers also concerned themselves with humbler, equally unpleasant, problems. During the 1914–1918 World War a Cambridge zoologist, A.E. Shipley, had published *The Minor Horrors of War,* a small book dealing with the house fly, the bed-bug, the flea, the louse and similar creatures. It was followed by a second volume covering other vermin. As a result the Museum was inundated with enquires. It responded, firstly by producing a series of Economic Pamphlets such as *A Guide to Rats and Mice as Enemies of Mankind,* which offered advice on how to deal with such pests, and, secondly, by appointing a member of staff, Frederick Laing, who spent the next thirty years dealing solely with entomological enquiries of a medical and economic nature.

The history of the Museum's research is punctuated by advances based on the availability and application of new technology. Many of these advances have been minor or restricted to specialized areas of study but a very few have enabled researchers to make a quantum leap in understanding by opening up new worlds of information. One of these innovations, the electron microscope, had an impact on almost all areas of Museum research.

The first electron microscope was constructed in the 1930s and the Museum purchased its first model, a transmission electron microscope, in 1965. The then Director, Gordon Frank Claringbull, believed that Museum scientists would benefit from access to this latest technological advance, and so it proved. Conventional microscopes use light focused by lenses to allow the examination of specimens. The most powerful can magnify an object up to a thousand times before clarity and resolution is lost. The electron microscope uses a beam of electrons focused by electro-magnets to illuminate the object and magnify objects up to a million times. The first commercially available models were transmission electron microscopes, which directed a beam of electrons through ultra thin sections and projected an image of the specimen onto a fluorescent screen. By 1967, scanning electron microscopes (SEMs) were becoming established and the Museum installed its first SEM that same year. They utilize a scanned beam of electrons to excite the electrons from the sample surface, which create an image of the sample on a screen. This tremendous leap forward in technology enabled whole objects to be viewed for the first time at ultra-high magnifications. Now, features were revealed that before had been obscure or invisible. The results were often very beautiful, sometimes breathtaking and always enlightening. The intricate architecture of pollen grains, the sense organs of butterflies and details of dinosaur teeth were revealed in all their glory!

All branches of the natural sciences took up the new technology with gusto. The new dimension allowed previously unobservable characters to be used in interpreting specimens and led to ground-breaking research, particularly in diatoms. These single-celled organisms have a shell-like casing of silica and the precise arrangement of pores, ridges and other structures are the basis for their classification. Under the ultimately discriminating lens of the electron microscope, diatoms which at lower resolution can appear similar, are seen to be quite different and to represent separate species.

The only drawbacks to scanning electron microscopy are the need to coat the specimen with a fine layer of gold to make it conductive of the electron beam and the necessity to view the specimen in a vacuum. Electrons are readily absorbed in air but behave very much like light in a vacuum. The coating renders the specimen unsuitable for more conventional examination techniques.

....

Prior to 1930 organisms such as diatoms were studied exclusively with light microscopes. Modern electron microscopes reveal even greater detail of the silica shells of these minute organisms.

Types and other unique or important specimens could not be studied in this way. Following further development of the SEM, the Museum obtained an even more advanced model in 1979, an environmental scanning electron microscope, which allows specimens to be scanned without first being gold-plated. Using this machine, even type specimens can be examined and returned unaltered to the collections, an advantage unique to Museum researchers since The Natural History Museum was the only institute of its kind to use such technology. The Museum was at the forefront of the application of this technique, which is now an established benchmark used by microscopists worldwide.

The War years of 1939–1945 put a temporary stop to many of the research activities, and the period immediately afterwards was one of reconstruction. It was in the 1960s that research really began to expand, with staff numbers rising by over one-third of the pre-War level. One event from this period is particularly noteworthy for its effect on research in one part of the Museum.

. . . .

The Museum did not escape the War entirely unscathed. In September 1940 a strike by oil and incendiary bombs caused considerable damage to the Botany Department and its collections.

The Department of Botany and the Royal Botanic Gardens at Kew both maintained large herbaria. Despite generally cordial relations between the staff of the two institutes they were, in practice, rivals. Indeed, there had been several attempts in the past to merge the collections under the auspices of Kew, all of them stoutly rebuffed by the Museum. In 1961 a division of responsibility, which became known as the Morton Agreement after the chairman of the review body proposing it, was accepted by the two institutes. The purpose of this accord was to prevent duplication of taxonomic research and acquisition of specimens. In effect, the Department of Botany and Kew divided the world between them. The Department would deal principally with plants from Europe, northwest Africa, North and Central America, and the Arctic and Antarctic regions; Kew would have the remainder. In geographical terms the Department appeared to get the worst of the deal, but this division applied only to flowering plants and ferns. As part of the agreement, the Department became solely responsible for all algae, mosses and lichens.

The continued expansion into new fields of interest, together with the availability of new technology and increasing specialization, brought its own dangers. The need to organize the Museum's research into a new, more focused pattern became apparent. The new approach, dating from 1990, was to organize research projects into 'Themes' based on the nature of the research being pursued rather than the organisms studied, as had previously been the case. The aims were to enable experts in separate but related fields to keep in closer touch with each other's work and to present that work to the outside world in a clearer and simpler way. Thus the Faunas and Floras Theme contains projects based in the Departments of Botany, Entomology and Zoology but all concerned with the task of describing the animals and plants of different regions. The number of Themes varies over time and at the time of writing stands at eight: Biomedical Sciences; Earth Materials, History and Processes; Ecological Patterns and Processes; Faunas and Floras; Soil Biodiversity; Systematics and Evolution; Collections Management; Facilities Provision. Their titles, together with the number of individual research projects – almost 700 are ongoing – give some idea of the breadth of research in the Museum today. This thematic approach better reflects the trend of modern research, which involves teams of specialists collaborating on a single project or combining different skills for a multidisciplinary attack on a problem.

. . . .
Daniel Solander
apponted to the
staff in 1773, was
the museum's
omly qualified
scientist.

Recruitment of Museum staff had always been somewhat esoteric. Appointments had been made by the Principal Trustees ever since the foundation of the British Museum in 1753. The deed of appointment of Daniel Solander as Under-Librarian (now in the Owen Collection, General Library) declares that "Now we Thomas Archbishop of Canterbury, Robert Earl of Northington, Lord High Chancellor, and Sir John Cost Barb Speaker, by virtue and in pursuance of the said act Have nominated and appointed and by these presents Do nominate and appoint Daniel Solander Doctor of Physick to be one of these said three assistants. To hold and execute the said imployment and service of an assistant according to the true intent and meaning of the said act. Given under our hands this said ninth day of July one thousand seven hundred and sixty five."

The language was simpler at the end of the 19th century, but nothing else much had changed. When a new assistant botanist was needed to replace William Fawcett in 1887, word of the vacancy was passed to friendly university departments so that the professors could spread the word to any good chaps looking for a job. Intending candidates had to fill in an application form that began with the words "I beg most respectfully to offer myself as a candidate ...", and send it, along with letters of testimonial and recommendation, to the Archbishop of Canterbury. The Archbishop next convened the meeting of the Principal Trustees referred to above, and the three men, none of whom knew a carpel from a stamen, sifted through the applications to produce a shortlist of "nominated" candidates. These lucky nominees could then compete for the post by taking a Civil Service examination in things like writing from dictation, orthography and translation from Latin. An enquiry was then made to ensure that the winner was "free from any physical defect or disease which would interfere with the proper discharge of his duties", and, all being well, he would be appointed by the Trustees. This bizarre system survived almost unchanged until 1939.

When it first opened its doors in South Kensington in 1881 the Museum had a staff of 109. Fifty-seven of these were concerned with the day-to-day functions of a large public building, including fourteen labourers, stokers for the boilers, window cleaners, a locksmith, a plumber and a ladies' attendant. The Museum even had its own Superintendent of Fire Engines and the splendidly titled "Engineer in charge of the Warming and Ventilating Apparatus"! By contrast, the science staff numbered only fifty-two (including the twenty-two members of the Department of Zoology who were still based in Bloomsbury). In addition to the Superintendent, they consisted of four Keepers or Heads of Department, one Assistant Keeper, eight 1st Class Assistants and ten 2nd Class Assistants, all of whom carried out research in addition to other duties such as administration. The twenty-eight Attendants and Boy Attendants served in more mundane capacities in the various departments.

. . . .
The cleaning staff outside the museum prior to an outing in the 1890's.

The 13
Attendants
and three
Boy Attendants
of the Zoology
Department
in 1885.

. . . .
Lucy Evelyn
Cheeseman on
a collecting trip
to Papua New
Guinea.

Given the extent of the collections the number of science staff was not high and the keepers were continually requesting expansion of the staff to cope with the work expected of their departments. These requests were frequently refused or lagged well behind the need for them, but the problem was somewhat cushioned by the existence of another group of individuals. These were the unofficial workers, a very broad term that covered a disparate array of individuals who fell, quite literally, into two classes. The first class were people of independent means who pursued their interests in natural history among the Museum's collections. Many were or became researchers renowned for their expertise in particular groups of organisms. An example is Frederick Vincent Theobald who, despite spending many years working in the Museum as a world authority on mosquitoes, was never actually employed there. Some volunteers contributed in other ways, for example Miss Lucy Evelyn Cheeseman travelled to remote parts of the world between 1924 and 1955 to make important collections of animals, plants and insects that she donated to the Museum. The second class was rather different. Although referred to as volunteers, they were actually part-time employees who were paid low hourly rates for specific pieces of work. At times the total number of volunteers exceeded that of the staff. Enthusiastic and unencumbered by administrative duties, they were often extremely productive, and both groups made valuable contributions to Museum science.

Today the number of Museum staff stands at 721, of whom approximately 260 are scientists devoting the majority of their time to the collections and research, while a further 58 provide library and information services. There are still two classes of unofficial workers, although they are no longer distinguished by their incomes. Volunteers (unpaid) have a general interest and work wherever help is required; associates pursue specific research interests of their own but which are complementary with those of the Museum.

In addition to these two groups of individuals the Museum has always maintained symbiotic relationships with independent scientific bodies. In some cases the link is physical in that staff of certain organizations whose work is closely connected with that of the Museum do actually work in the building. The Commonwealth Institute of Entomology, the Zoological Record, the Botanical Society of the British Isles and the British Geological Survey are but a few examples of past and present partners.

. . . . . .
Museum scientists train local people in many countries to collect specimens and survey biodiversity.

ARCHAEOPTERYX

In 1860 the description of a single, fossilized feather in a letter to a German mineralogy journal heralded a major palaeontological discovery.

The fossilized feather had been found by Hermann von Meyer in a quarry in Bavaria, but the crucial specimen was owned by another collector. In return for medical services to them and their families, the quarrymen at Lagenaltheim gave any fossils they found to the local doctor, Karl Haberlein. They must have been sharp-eyed, for Haberlein built up a varied collection of 1703 fossils. Among them was a reptile-like creature discovered in 1861 in which the skeleton and impressions of feathers were almost perfectly preserved. This "feathered fossil" was *Archaeopteryx lithographica*.

On hearing of Haberlein's collection in 1862, the British Museum's Superintendent Richard Owen and George Robert Waterhouse, Keeper of Geology, immediately began negotiations to purchase some or all of it, with *Archaeopteryx* the prize. The miserliness of the British Museum's Trustees initially prevented them from meeting Haberlein's estimation of the collection's value of £700 and the negotiations appeared doomed. However, a compromise was reached under which the bulk of the collection, including *Archaeopteryx*, was purchased immediately with the remainder bought the following year.

Why was the British Museum so keen to obtain this single specimen? Its importance was immediately obvious and eminent scientists queued to examine it. In 1864, John Ruskin described the specimen as "one unique as an example for a species (a whole Kingdom of unknown living creatures being announced by that fossil)". The fossil in question was of a small, dinosaur-like animal about the size of a magpie. It had a long bony tail, clawed fingers and toothed jaws like a reptile, but a wishbone and feathers, both features unique to birds. Was it a bird? Was it a reptile? Was it a missing link between the two? All three answers were to be put forward by different authorities, but what was certain was the existence of powerful evidence for evolution. Owen was critical of Darwin's evolutionary theory but, to his credit, he not only insisted upon purchasing the specimen but made a careful and accurate study of it. Modern scientists accept *Archaeopteryx* as the first bird. This begs the question, from which group did *Archaeopteryx* evolve? Early suggestions included various primitive reptiles, and in 1986 research suggested the group of small carnivorous dinosaurs that includes *Velociraptor* and *Deinonychus* as the ancestral group.

Controversy has several times hovered around *Archaeopteryx*. The latest occurred in 1985 when the distinguished astronomers Professors Sir Fred Hoyle and Chandra Wickramasinghe declared that the London specimen had been faked by Karl Haberlein by the cunning addition of feather impressions on a limestone paste around a genuine dinosaur skeleton. They also accused the Museum of knowingly covering up the forgery and of even enhancing it by adding features including extra feather impressions. Museum scientists were quick to refute the charges point by point, and the more recent discovery of two more fossils of *Archaeopteryx* to add to the five already known completed the rebuttal.

CHAPTER 8

THE DIGITAL AGE:
INTO THE FUTURE

The first computer delivered to the South Kensington site arrived in 1979 but the Museum had dipped its toes into the digital waters some years earlier. The statistical analysis of biological data, or biometrics, was not a new approach, but the use of computers in numerical taxonomy developed during the 1950s and 1960s. The few such research studies carried out within the Museum at that time had utilized computer facilities elsewhere. However, the possibilities offered by computers in terms of curation and collections management had also been recognized. The Museum's Report for 1966–1968 contained an article considering this aspect of the technology and advocating the replacement of unwieldy card-catalogues relating to the collections with a computerized system. To make his point that Museum scientists faced a formidable task in dealing with both the biological data in the collections and the steadily increasing amount of published information, the author had quoted an example from two works published at the beginning of the decade. This claimed that "the amount of information in a mammalian nucleus would, if set in type, fill a thousand standard text books, and that the information contained in the ten million books of the Library of Congress ... could, if encoded, be comfortably stored in the anther of a lily". A little over-the-top perhaps, but an evocative portrayal of the situation. At the time computers were somewhat primitive machines that used information stored on punched cards or tape – a Friden "Flexowriter" for producing paper tape had been installed in the Museum – and were scarcely less unwieldy than the index-card systems they were intended to replace. Nonetheless, when the Trustees agreed on 11th December 1969 to an investigation into the use of computers they opened the door to a new information age in the Museum.

Laboratories equipped with the latest technology are an integral part of the Museum's research facilities.

Initially computer use was centralized. Equipment was relatively expensive and expertise thin on the ground, but computer technology advanced rapidly and the advent of desktop computers saw these machines springing up in all departments. To provide a system linking the many different users, miles of cabling had to be installed. This was no easy matter in a structure as old and complex as the Waterhouse building, but the effort and expense were worthwhile and use of the new technology gained momentum. The Department of Library Services, for example, engaged in computerizing the entire stock of books and journals, a truly mammoth task that began in 1986 and is still ongoing. Around 300,000 entries have been completed and the eventual total is estimated at 400,000 titles. Various collection databases were set up in different departments to record details of specimens, and researchers made extensive use of computers in fields such as DNA analysis. Today it is hardly surprising that computers are an essential part of everyday life in the Museum, from handling financial administration to recording loans of specimens, from analysing satellite images to providing exhibition displays, yet some of the old card-catalogues remain. Despite considerable effort, the task of capturing all of the data in the Museum's collections in electronic form is far from complete and will continue well into the future.

. . . .

In the pre-computer age the heart of the Museum's communication system was the telephone exchange, shown here in 1933.

As well as internal benefits, information technology brought external ones too. Scientists rarely work in isolation. They need access to collections and literature outside their home institute and, equally important, contact with colleagues with similar interests elsewhere in the world. What they needed was a cheap, instant form of communication as a means of sharing information. Together, email and the World Wide Web provided it. Using these technologies scientists are able to communicate regularly, discuss and disseminate ideas and trade information with a speed and facility previously unavailable. There were wider benefits too, since the World Wide Web offered an interface with the outside world. Now, those visitors making the journey to South Kensington need not be the only audience for the Museum's unique services. Exhibition and educational materials could be offered to those unable to come in person and access to the treasure trove of information in the collections, previously somewhat restricted, could be made available on a global scale.

Funding for the Museum has always been vexatious. Maintaining a large building, mounting exhibitions, curating and researching vast collections and buying huge quantities of books, not to mention paying the staff, clearly requires large amounts of money. Government funding, on which the Museum relied, varied with the economic and political climate. The 1960s were a generally favourable time, but towards the end of the decade the Museum was becoming uneasy about the level of its funding. Unknowing, it

. . . .
A Museum scientist uses a computer and satellite data to record information in the forests of Belize.

was soon to enter a lean period lasting some twenty years. Declining Government funding and increasingly tight budgets required an increasing number of cutbacks. As the situation worsened, the Director and Trustees deemed their least damaging option to be a reduction in the level of work across the whole spectrum of Museum activities. This decision did not signify a passive acceptance of the situation. During the 1980s in particular,

. . . .

After an earlier false start, admission charges were imposed in 1985.

various new fund-raising strategies were explored and many put into effect. Admission charges, which had been forced on the Museum by the Government for a few months in 1974 before being abandoned, were reluctantly reintroduced in 1985. The souvenir and book shops were expanded and the building was hired out for commercial functions – dining beneath the dinosaurs in the Central Hall was and still is popular. Museum publications sold well and generated considerable income. In 1987 a special charity was set up, the Development Trust, to facilitate sponsorship for activities ranging from field work to new exhibitions and conservation of the collections, and a year later a new Department of Marketing and Development was created to market the Museum in all its aspects to its many audiences. The scientists took on increasing numbers of commercial contracts, especially in the expanding field of environmental impact assessments that monitored the effects on the environment in projects such as the building of the Channel Tunnel. By 1989, 20% of all income came from such commercial sources. Successful as they were in enabling the Museum to generate additional funds, these assorted efforts were not enough to stave off the unkindest cut of all and in 1990 the Museum was forced to take extreme measures. For the first time in its history, redundancies were announced. Eighty-three posts, representing a tenth of the total staff, were lost, some fifty of them from the science departments.

Although the situation was hardly unusual for the time – many people in other walks of life suffered a similar fate – it was a severe blow to the Museum. Whole areas of research were abandoned because of lack of expertise, parts of the collections were relegated to care and maintenance basis only, and new exhibitions were put on hold. However, the institute proved to be a tough survivor and recovery took much less time than was feared so that within two years staff numbers were back to pre-1990 levels. The legacy was a noticeable change in Museum culture.

Future areas for research were chosen using even more rigorous criteria to determine their scientific relevance, resources more strictly controlled and the justification required for new posts made tougher. Above all, fund-raising is now a permanent part of Museum life. In 2000 the Museum raised 39% of its income through self-generated funds while maintaining a balance between purely scientific and educational activities and commercial ones.

It was during this difficult period that a significant change in the Museum's image occurred. The South Kensington site had spent the previous 107 years as the British Museum (Natural History), a name that simultaneously implied its genesis and confused many visitors who came expecting to see Egyptian mummies and other artefacts of ancient civilizations. In 1988 a new name was acquired, The Natural History Museum. There was considerable debate over the precise form of these four words. Was inclusion of the definite article a little arrogant, implying this was the only museum of natural history in the world? Should the word British appear to indicate this was a national and not a local institute, or London to give a clue as to its location? Perhaps with hindsight this was all a little silly, but by the nature of their work museum scientists take the accurate application of names very seriously. Eventually agreement was reached on a title that the public, anyway, had been using informally for many years.

. . . .
Staff protest against admission charges outside the Museum.

The last ten years of the 20th century encompassed changes both in the physical structure of the Museum and in the way it carries out its work. The public face has seen the development of a new set of exhibitions, including Ecology and the immensely popular Dinosaurs, as well as the transformation of the old Geological Museum into the Earth Galleries. The year 1993 saw the establishment of a wildlife garden at South Kensington, while at the other extreme the Las Cuevas Research Station has been developed in Belize to provide a permanent facility for tropical field work. Development of the South Kensington site to provide better accommodation brought a new Biomedical Centre and a combined Electron Microscope and Mineral Analysis Suite. Some of the most historically important botany collections, principally the Sloane

The Wildlife Garden is a popular outdoor exhibit. Since its establishment in 1993 several species of insects and plants not previously recorded in Central London have appeared there.

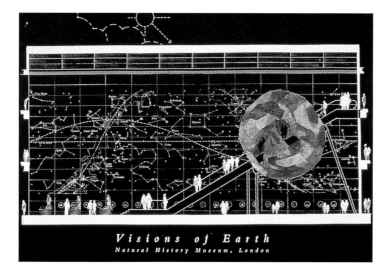

Visions of Earth
Natural History Museum, London

Herbarium, have been rehoused in environmentally controlled and secure conditions. New collections continue to pour into the Museum, and the results of research to flow out.

What of the future? Beyond the usual generalities, some trends and events can be predicted with a degree of certainty because they are already in train. "Nature abhors a vacuum" is an old phrase used to denote the fact that nature is in a continuous state of change. While this remains so, there will be scientists wishing to study it and an audience eager to have the results interpreted and presented to them. The focus for much of the research in the Museum in the near future can be summed up in two words, biodiversity and bioinformatics. Biodiversity was coined in the 1980s and refers to the taxonomic and functional diversity of living organisms, but its rise to prominence dates from 1992 when government representatives of 152 countries met in Rio de Janeiro to agree to the Convention on Biological Diversity. This global initiative recognized the need to catalogue and understand the living world in order to conserve precious natural resources for both the present and future generations. Meeting the requirements of the Convention has re-invigorated

. . . .
Establishing the new Earth Galleries involved installation of some large scale, spectacular and expensive exhibits. 'Visions of Earth', with the globe and escalator against a backdrop of constellations, required extensive planning.

. . . .
The Museum's field station is based at Las Cuevas, Belize, in one of the largest and best preserved areas of forest remaining in Central America.

An entomologist
in the field
records night-
flying insects
attracted by a
lamp as a means
of providing
an inventory of
the fauna.

traditional taxonomic and systematic research, which was in
danger of being overshadowed by other disciplines. Clearly,
before we can contemplate conserving or using the natural world
in a sustainable way, we first need to describe and catalogue it.
Probably few surprises lie in wait among the higher levels of
classification, but at the species level – "the parish registers
of life" – it is estimated that only 5% of living things are already
known to science. There is still much to do. The drawers and
cabinets of institutes such as the Museum contain a wealth of
information dating from hundreds of years ago to the present,
a truly unique source for investigating biodiversity and change.
At a different, more fundamental, level research into the molecular
and genetic aspects of life also contributes to our understanding
of biodiversity and these, too, fall within the Museum's remit.
One aspect that the traditional and modern approaches have in
common is the huge amount of data they generate. Bioinformatics
is a term dating from the 1990s and describes everything to

do with storing, handling and communicating biological data. Recording this data and making it readily available is a suitable challenge for the digital age.

Two further challenges for the Museum have already been anticipated. The first was dubbed "space, the eternal problem" by the eminent botanist William T. Stearn in his book *The Natural History Museum at South Kensington* in 1981, and despite additions, expansions and development since then the Museum is bursting at the seams. The second is the need for even greater access to the specimens and knowledge stored there. Consideration of these issues is behind the next phase of development. In an ambitious move, a completely new set of buildings, named the Darwin Centre after the great man of science, is being created in two phases on the South Kensington site. The first opened in 2001 and houses the wet collections, mainly of the Department of Zoology; the second, at the time of writing, is still in the planning stage and will eventually accommodate the Departments of Botany and Entomology. Improved conditions for the collections and research will be combined with better access, both physical and virtual, allowing the public to share in this heritage to an extent greater than ever before. In its mission the Museum will continue fulfilling Sloane's original intention when he bequeathed his wonderful collection to the nation, that it "may be rendered as useful as possible, as well towards satisfying the desire of the curious, as for the improvement of knowledge, and information of all persons".

. . . .
The Tank Room in the new Darwin Building houses the largest specimens stored in spirit, such as Komodo dragons and swordfish. Special lifting gear enables easier handling of large and unwieldy specimens.

. . . .
Moving specimen jars from the New Spirit Building for relocation in the Darwin Building.

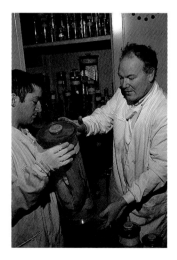

Central Hall Statues

Darwin came first. He was placed on the landing of the main staircase and unveiled on 9th June 1885, just four years after the Museum opened. He presided over the Hall in isolation for twelve years, no doubt watching the progress of William Henry Flower's evolutionary exhibits with approval. In 1897 he was joined by the bronze statue of Sir Richard Owen, which was placed at the south end of the Hall, facing Darwin. The two men had not had much to say to each other in life, so it is not surprising that their statues appeared to glare at each other. In 1895 Darwin's old friend Thomas Huxley had died, and it was by now inevitable that a Memorial Committee should be set up with the aim of collecting money to provide a statue for the Museum. The Huxley appeal was the best supported of the three, raising £3378, of which £1813 was spent on a marble statue, which was unveiled on the east side of Central Hall on 23rd April 1900. Over the next few years memorials of one kind or another to Sir William Henry Flower, Frederick C. Selous, Alfred R. Wallace and to Messrs Godman and Salvin were unveiled, making the Central Hall a Valhalla for British natural history.

Originally seated on the main staircase, Darwin now presides over the North Hall.

By the 1920s the Hall had become something of a muddle. Darwin had always looked silly on the staircase as, viewed from below, his boots were far too prominent, while Owen was surrounded by exhibits and Huxley seemed more or less forgotten. The move of an Indian elephant to the Hall in 1927 meant that something had to make way to accommodate it. The Director's Solution, approved by the Trustees, was to put Owen on the staircase and have Darwin and Huxley facing each other from side bays near the Museum entrance. The proposal caused pandemonium.

·········
Bust of Selous.
The bas-relief
below depicts
African big game
and relates to
his career as
a hunter.

·········
Bronze statue
of Sir Richard
Owen.

Protests were led by Professor E.B. Poulton, an Oxford zoologist and one-time trustee, who opened a petition among Fellows of the Royal Society, begging the Trustees to change their minds and retain Darwin in his exalted position "as evidence that Mr Darwin's views have received your official sanction". The petition ends: "Restore the statue of the greatest naturalist the world has ever known to the one and only appropriate position in the building". The Archbishop of Canterbury became agitated ... questions were being asked!

Well, the storm in the teacup subsided and the moves were made, and when the two statues were moved to the North Hall in 1970 nobody made a sound. But it was hot while it lasted.

FURTHER READING

Banks, Sir Joseph (1743-1820), 1999. *The Endeavour journal of Joseph Banks, 25 Aug 1768 to 12 Jul 1771*. 2 volumes, arranged by B.P. Sandford. Mitchell Library, State Library of New South Wales, Sydney.

Cadbury, Deborah, 2000. *The dinosaur hunters : a true story of scientific rivalry and the discovery of the prehistoric world*. Fourth Estate, London, 384pp.

Cunningham, Colin, 2001. *The terracotta designs of Alfred Waterhouse*. Wiley-Academy, London, 192pp.

Dean, Dennis R., (ed.), 1999. *The first dinosaur book : Richard Owen on British fossil reptiles (1842)*. Scholars', Facsimiles, & Reprints, NY, 212pp.

Dept.Public Services in association with Dept. Palaeontology, The Natural History Museum, 1987. *The Feathers fly : is Archaeopteryx a fake?* The Natural History Museum, London, 16pp.

Gascoigne, John, 1994. *Joseph Banks and the English enlightenment : useful knowledge and polite culture*. Cambridge University Press, Cambridge, 324pp.

Girouard, Mark, 1999. *Alfred Waterhouse and The Natural History Museum*. The Natural History Museum, London, 64pp.

Gruber, Jacob W. and Thackray, John C., 1992. *Richard Owen commemoration : three studies*. The Natural History Museum, London, 181pp.

The guide, 1998. The Natural History Museum, London, 40pp.

Gunther, Albert Everard, 1980. *The founders of science at the British Museum 1753-1900*. Halesworth Press, Suffolk, 219pp.

McGirr, Nicola, 2000. *Nature's connections : an exploration of natural history*. The Natural History Museum, London, 212pp.

Musgrave, Toby, 1998. *The plant hunters : two hundred years of adventure and discovery around the world*. Ward Lock, London, 224pp.

Patterson, Colin, 1999. *Evolution*, 2nd edn. The Natural History Museum, London, 166pp.

Rice, A. L., 1999. *Voyages of discovery : three centuries of natural history exploration*. Scriptum Editions, London, 336pp.

Rupke, Nicolaas A., 1994. *Richard Owen : Victorian naturalist*. Yale University Press, London/New Haven, 462pp.

Ruse, Michael, 1999. *The Darwinian revolution : science red in tooth and claw*, 2nd edn. University of Chicago Press, Chicago, 346pp.

Shipman. P., 1998. *Taking wing : Archaeopteryx and the evolution of bird flight*. Simon & Schuster, New York, 336pp.

Smith, Christopher U. M., 1998. *Owen and Huxley : unfinished business*. In *Endeavour*, Vol. 22, no. 3, pp.110-113.

Stearn, W.T., 1998. *The Natural History Museum at South Kensington : a history of the Museum, 1753-1980*. The Natural History Museum, London, 414pp.

Unnatural history : a Victorian Society report on the internal alterations to the principal galleries of the Natural History Museum, South Kensington, 1992. Victorian Society, [1],8,[11] leaves, The Natural History Museum, London.

Whitehead, P.J.P., 1969. The Reeves collection of Chinese fish drawings. *Bulletin of the British Museum (Natural History)*, Historical Series 3, pp.191-233.

Whitehead, P. J. P. & Edwards, P. I., 1974. *Chinese natural history drawings : selected from the Reeves collection in the British Museum (Natural History) by Reeves, John, 1774-1856*. The Natural History Museum, London, 109pp. (Limited edn. of 400.)

Whitehead P. & Keates, C., 1981. *The British Museum (Natural History)*. Scala Books, London, 128pp.

admission charges 130
Anning, Mary 34
Antiquities, Department of (British Museum) 29
Archaeopteryx 124-5
Ashcroft, Frederick Noel, collection of Swiss minerals 78-9

Banks, Sir Joseph 26, 27, 38
Banksia serrata 26
Baryonix walkeri 81-2
beetle specimens 68
Belize, Las Cuevas Research Station 132, 133
biodiversity, research into 133-4
bioinformatics 134-5
biology *see* botany collections; Human Biology Hall; zoology collections
birds *see* ornithology
blackflies 108
research into 115-16
blue whale 103
Board of Trustees (British Museum) 33, 47
and establishment of the Natural History Museum 55-6
and purchase of the Sloane collection 18, 19
Board of Trustees (for Sloane), and sale of Sloane's collection 17-19
bones *see* osteology
botany collections 20-1, 38-9, 101, 132-3
Botany Department 119, 135
Botany, Department of (British Museum) 50
Botany Gallery 99
British Museum
in the 1850s 48-9
criticisms of 29, 30, 33, 42-3, 47, 55
Department of Antiquities 29
Department of Botany 50
Department of Geology 42, 50

Department of Manuscripts 23
Department of Mineralogy 50
Department of Natural and Artificial Production 23
Department of Natural History 39, 50, 55-6
Department of Natural History and Modern Curiosities 29
Department of Printed Books 23, 39
Department of Zoology 41, 50, 55
early development 23-5, 27-30, 33
establishment of 17-19
Natural History Galleries 44-6, 47-8
new building 37-9
review of (1835) 33, 35, 42, 55
visitors' access 24-5, 29, 48
see also Board of Trustees (British Museum)
British Museum Act (1753) 19, 69
British Museum (Natural History) *see* Natural History Museum
Brown, Robert 38-9, 40
Buckland, William 34

Calman, William 74-5
Carnegie, Andrew 101-2
Carruthers, William 40
catalogues 14-15, 27, 42, 43, 109-10
Central Hall 59, 62-3, 65, 66-7, 95, 96-7, 136-9
Cheeseman, Lucy 122
Children, John George 30, 33, 41
Children's Centre 105
chocolate 13-14, 15
cladistics 113-14
see also evolution
Claringbull, Gordon 116-17
computers 127-9

conservation 89
see also species conservation
Cook, James 27
Courten, William 14
curation 109

Darwin, Charles 136-7
Darwin Centre 91, 135
Dawson, Charles 84
dinosaurs 34-5, 49, 81-2, 101-2
Diplodocus 101-2
diseases, research into 115-16
displays, design of 93-101

Earth Galleries 82, 104, 105, 132, 133
education
museum work in 103-7
see also displays; guide books; Guide Lecturer
Edward VII 101
Egerton, Sir Phillip 47
electron microscopes 116-18, 132
Elgin Marbles 29, 37
Ellis, Sir Henry (Principal Librarian) 33, 47, 49
entomology *see* insect collections; medical entomology
Entomology Department 119, 135
environmental scanning microscopes 118
evolution 112-13, 124-5
expeditions 27, 74-5

Fawcett, William 120
Fish Gallery 98
Flower, Sir William 100
Forshall, Josiah 33
fossil collection 34-5, 42, 49, 64-5, 69-70, 81-2, 84, 101-2, 124-5
Fowke, Francis 59
fraudulent specimens 84-5
funding problems 129-31

Geological Museum 82-4